Teach This Poem, Volume I

Instill a love of poetry in your classroom with the illuminating and inviting lesson plans from Teach This Poem classroom activities. Co-published with the Academy of American Poets, the leading champion of poets and poetry in the US, this book is an accessible entry-point to teaching poetry and fostering a poetic sensibility in the classroom. Each lesson follows a consistent format, with a warm-up activity to introduce the chosen poem, pair-shares, whole class synthesis, related resources, oral readings, and extension activities. Curated by the AAP, the poems are chosen with an eye toward fostering compassion and representing diverse experiences. Understanding that poetry is a powerful way of seeing the world, the volumes are organized thematically: Volume I is centered on the natural world and Volume II on equality and justice. Aligned with current standards and pedagogy, the lessons in these poems will inspire English teachers and their students alike.

Madeleine Fuchs Holzer was the Inaugural Educator in Residence at the Academy of American Poets, where she curated and created Teach This Poem. She has taught at the high school and university levels, and has worked as an arts-in-education administrator. Her poetry and essays have appeared in several literary journals.

Founded in 1934 in New York City by Marie Bullock, the **Academy of American Poets** is an organization that connects millions of readers to poets' work with its many free programs and publications. Its mission is to support poets at all stages of their careers and to foster the appreciation of contemporary poetry.

Teach This Poem, Volume I
The Natural World

Madeleine Fuchs Holzer
The Academy of American Poets

NEW YORK AND LONDON

First published 2024
by Routledge
605 Third Avenue, New York, NY 10158

and by Routledge
4 Park Square, Milton Park, Abingdon, Oxon, OX14 4RN

Routledge is an imprint of the Taylor & Francis Group, an informa business

© 2024 Madeleine Fuchs Holzer and The Academy of American Poets

The right of Madeleine Fuchs Holzer and The Academy of American Poets to be identified as authors of this work has been asserted in accordance with sections 77 and 78 of the Copyright, Designs and Patents Act 1988.

All rights reserved. No part of this book may be reprinted or reproduced or utilised in any form or by any electronic, mechanical, or other means, now known or hereafter invented, including photocopying and recording, or in any information storage or retrieval system, without permission in writing from the publishers.

Trademark notice: Product or corporate names may be trademarks or registered trademarks, and are used only for identification and explanation without intent to infringe.

ISBN: 978-1-032-52925-7 (hbk)
ISBN: 978-1-032-52145-9 (pbk)
ISBN: 978-1-003-40921-2 (ebk)

DOI: 10.4324/9781003409212

Typeset in Univers
by SPi Technologies India Pvt Ltd (Straive)

Contents

Preface by Richard Blanco	vii
Introduction by Madeleine Fuchs Holzer	ix

Chapter 1 *Why Poetry?* — 1

Introduction	1
"These Poems" by June Jordan	2
"There is no frigate like a book (1263)" by Emily Dickinson	5
"From WHEREAS ["WHEREAS when offered…"]" by Layli Long Soldier	7
"Poetry" by Marianne Moore	10
"Valentine for Ernest Mann" by Naomi Shihab Nye	13
"Bracken" by Kai Carlson-Wee	16
"On Gathering Artists" by Alberto Ríos	18
"The Indications [excerpt]" by Walt Whitman	21
"A Way of Seeing" by Kwame Dawes	23

Chapter 2 *The Natural World* — 26

Introduction	26
Part 1: Future	27
"Letter to Someone Living Fifty Years From Now" by Matthew Olzmann	27
"Characteristics of Life" by Camille T. Dungy	30
"The Everglades" by Campbell McGrath	33
"The Shapes of Leaves" by Arthur Sze	35
"The Forest for the Trees" by Rena Priest	37
"Dead Stars" by Ada Limón	39
"Radium Dream" by Sheila Black	42
"Nimbawaadaan Akiing / I Dream A World" by Margaret Noodin	44
Part 2: Present	47
"In Praise of Okra" by January Gill O'Neil	47
"Remember" by Joy Harjo	50
"The Tree Sparrows" by Joseph O. Legaspi	53
"A Small Needful Fact" by Ross Gay	55
"In cold spring air" by Reginald Gibbons	57
"Cherry Blossoms" by Toi Derricotte	59
"Map" by Linda Hogan	62

"She Was Fed Turtle Soup" by Lois Red Elk	65
"Instructions on Not Giving Up" by Ada Limón	68
"The Silver Thread" by Afaa Michael Weaver	70
"Complaint of El Rio Grande" by Richard Blanco	73
Part 3: Past	76
"Coyote" by Alexander Posey	76
"Peace Path" by Heid E. Erdrich	79
"Binsey Poplars" by Gerard Manley Hopkins	82
"The Snowfall Is So Silent" by Miguel de Unamuno and translated by Ricardo Alberto Maldonado	84
"To Winter" by Claude McKay	88
"Maggie and Milly and Molly and May" by E. E. Cummings	90
"Willow Poem" by William Carlos Williams	92
"Saint Francis and the Sow" by Galway Kinnell	94
"The Metier of Blossoming" by Denise Levertov	96
"Blessing the boats" by Lucille Clifton	99

Chapter 3 *Glossary of Poetic Terms*   *101*

Types of Feet in Poetry	107
Types of Meter in Poetry	107
Four Examples of Quatrains in Poetry	110
Seven Examples of Repetition in Poetry	110
Types of Stanzas in Poetry	112

Chapter 4 *Teaching with Primary Sources*   *114*

"Ozymandias" by Percy Bysshe Shelley	115
Part 1: Finding a Resource	116
Part 2: Engaging Through Inquiry	117
Part 3: Choosing the Best Resource	118

Chapter 5 *Adapting Teach This Poem to an Online or Hybrid Classroom*   *119*
Academy of American Poets

Poet and Translator Biographies	121
Bibliography	128
Credits	132
Acknowledgments	136
Author Biography	137

Preface by Richard Blanco

Since my tenure as Presidential Inaugural Poet for Barack Obama, I've received thousands of messages and letters from people from all walks of life expressing how powerfully they had connected with the inaugural poem and been turned on to poetry. Moreover, over the past decade I've had the honor and privilege of sharing my love for poetry at hundreds of diverse venues, from government agencies to engineering and law firms, from grade schools and universities to advocacy groups of all kinds. I've witnessed people by the hundreds inspired by a newfound connection to poetry, suddenly understanding that poetry was not what they had thought it was. These positive reactions bolstered what I already believed to be true: poetry is indeed powerful and life-enriching. But they also highlighted a contradiction; after all, so many people have outright confessed to me that they just don't *get* poetry, don't care for it, even hate it. I recognized that there is a hidden hunger for poetry and an unrealized potential for this often misunderstood art.

Reflecting on my life, I recall that throughout my education I was never introduced to a single poem by a living poet. As a result, my classroom experience with poetry was lackluster and detached at best. Not until I began taking creative writing courses on my own after college did I encounter the incredible spectrum of contemporary poets. Poetry then became alive and relevant—it changed my life forever. But why hadn't that happened sooner? Why isn't poetry a larger part of our cultural lives, more connected to our popular conversations as with film, music, and novels? Why isn't poetry more entrenched in our history, rooted in our folklore, and established in our national identity as it is in other countries? Where's the disconnect?

I believe part of the reason has to do with education. The way poetry is generally taught (especially in K–12 grades), even by teachers who love poetry, falls short of exploring a rich engagement with the art. Of course there are wonderful teachers of poetry, but many teachers have been taught that poetry is mysterious—and like sleuths searching for the one correct, finite meaning of a poem, they believe that there is only one way to read a specific poem. As a result, these educators often acknowledge that they feel intimidated by poetry, and one can conclude that their students become similarly intimidated.

To this point, there exists a recognized fear or dislike of poetry: metrophobia. Many people first develop this phobia in classrooms when asked to rank poems according to artificial scales, to break them down, or to search for esoteric meanings. I believe that people who suffer from metrophobia were never properly introduced to poetry in the first place.

The Teach This Poem series of activities in this book are the perfect antidote for metrophobia. Created and curated by the ingenious and dedicated educator Madeleine Fuchs Holzer, these lesson plans provide an innovative, easy, and inviting approach to teaching poetry. I've used Teach This Poem activities at dozens of class visits to K–12 schools and universities, and I can attest to just how effective they are at converting students, even educators, into poetry lovers. In her introduction, Holzer discusses in depth the multi-faceted components of the series. There are several elements I've found especially important, original, and worth highlighting here. For instance, the interdisciplinary dimension of the activities, which helps students connect to and explore other fields of knowledge through poetry, makes poetry relevant beyond the language arts classroom. Also, activities often examine poems through the lens of craft, that is to say, how a poem is *made* through various craft components such as sensory details, imagery, rhythm, and figurative language. As a poet, I feel it's important for students, as well as educators, to consider how a poem is crafted in order to enhance their overall understanding of the art form. Lastly, the series is customizable; once teachers learn the general approach and framework, they can write their own activities using poems that they'd like to teach in order to meet the particular needs and interests of their students.

In closing, I'd be remiss if I didn't ask the pink-elephant-in-the room question: Why is poetry important? In my view, its importance can be boiled down to two fundamental reasons. First, and perhaps most obviously, through the study of poetry students achieve a greater mastery of language, and language is essential to the success of practically every human endeavor and relationship, whether personal or professional. Poetry also cultivates awareness and empathy, and a more aware and empathetic person benefits in every aspect of their life. I think of poems as mirrors in which lives blur together through language. In that blurring, we arrive at a more compassionate understanding of others and of ourselves, and thus, a better world for all of us. May this book help you and your students create that world through poetry.

Introduction by Madeleine Fuchs Holzer

Background

Teach This Poem is an extension of the Academy of American Poets' long history of providing educational resources to teachers that began when Robert Frost encouraged the organization's founder Marie Bullock to "get poetry into the high schools" in the 1960s. Shortly after, in 1966, the Academy launched the first Poets in the Schools program in partnership with the National Endowment for the Arts, which had been founded a year earlier. Thirty years later, the Academy launched Poets.org, which was originally intended to be an online poetry classroom and was shaped in consultation with the educational philosopher Maxine Greene. In 2014, Poets.org was redesigned and the flagship program Poem-a-Day was revamped to begin publishing new poems by the day's living poets, making Poets.org a rich source for contemporary poetry.

Seeking to strengthen and add to the educational content on Poets.org, in 2013 Jennifer Benka, then Executive Director of the Academy, asked me to write lesson plans along themes that were linked to each month. Each lesson included several poems from Poets.org, detailed experiential lessons with multiple entry points, and often interdisciplinary resources. To collect feedback on the lesson plans, during the 2013–2014 school year we organized a number of teacher meetups in partnership with the New York City Department of Education and New Visions for Public Schools. The meetups provided professional development for the teachers and important feedback for the Academy about how we might structure our future education efforts. At the last of these meetups, we asked the teachers how Poets.org could be even more helpful. One of the most active participants wondered if we could develop something like Poem-a-Day for teachers. She shared that the lessons I had developed were very useful, but too long for teachers who sometimes had very little time to read them. She suggested that a poem, an interdisciplinary resource, and some quick activities might be all they needed. A week later, Teach This Poem was born.

Like Poem-a-Day, Teach This Poem is emailed to subscribers free of charge, and is published and archived on Poets.org. Sent each Monday morning during the school year, Teach This Poem, as recommended to us, includes a poem, interdisciplinary resource, and several classroom activities. In response to further teacher input on the series, we have become more explicit about the philosophy behind the format and activities, added a More Context section, and provided extension activities to target different grade levels.

In 2018, Teach This Poem, which by then had grown to 30,000 subscribers, received the Innovations in Reading Prize from the National Book Foundation.

Philosophy

Teach This Poem is based on the idea that a "poetic sensibility" can be fostered in students, and that this sensibility will not only help students experience poetry more deeply, but also help them look more deeply at phenomena across academic disciplines. The philosophical foundation for developing a poetic sensibility comes from the writings of John Dewey (1980) and Maxine Greene (2018), and resonates with the writings of the poet Jane Hirshfield (2017) on the idea of "poetic perception."

According to Dewey:

> to perceive, a beholder must create his own experience. And his creation must include relations comparable to those which the original producer underwent...The artist selected, simplified, clarified, abridged and condensed according to his interest. The beholder must go through these operations according to his point of view and interest.
>
> (Dewey, 1980, p. 54)

Maxine Greene built on Dewey's idea of perception in her lectures at Lincoln Center Institute when she coined the phrase "Aesthetic Education." She defined this as:

> an intentional undertaking designed to nurture appreciative, reflective, cultural, participatory engagements with the arts by enabling learners to notice what there is to be noticed, and to lend works of art their lives in such a way that they can achieve them as variously meaningful. When this happens, new connections are made in experience; new patterns are formed, new vistas are opened.
>
> (Greene, 2018, p. 6)

Although neither Dewey nor Greene addressed the study of poetry as an art form directly, we have adapted their thoughts, while adding Jane Hirshfield's idea that poetic perception's work "is not simply the recording of inner or outer perception; it makes by words and music new possibilities of perceiving" (Hirshfield, 2015, p. 3). We propose that when someone deeply engages with poetry, they experience, through mind and sense connections, its meaning and emotional impact, and understand the experience *beyond the words*. When this happens, not only can they apply what they have learned to poetry, but to learning in other disciplines—their poetic perception becomes a poetic sensibility.

The characteristics of poetic sensibility include:

- Having a keen sensitivity to the surrounding world (multisensory perception)
- Asking questions
- Identifying patterns
- Making both intuitive and logical connections
- Having a facility and passion for finding the right word or phrase to express feelings and meaning
- Using imagination to connect these in unexpected ways.

More can be read about poetic sensibility in the essay "Poetic Sensibility: What It Is and Why We Need It in 21st Century Education," available on Poets.org.

Importantly, we also keep in mind that all classrooms are composed of participants from different communities, countries, ethnicities, races, and gender identities. We feature poems that are written primarily by living artists, and include poets who represent a wide range of backgrounds. It is important for participants to encounter poetry by people from their communities, especially those who might not be represented in older curricula and textbooks. We aim to offer participants fresh perspectives that will inform their understanding of current events, and we curate poems and resources that speak to today's most relevant issues.

We also curate Teach This Poem with an eye toward fostering empathy. As the poet Mark Doty once said while speaking about the role of the art form, "The project of poetry, in a way, is to raise language to such a level that it can convey the precise nature of subjective experience" (Doty, 2010). Poetry also encourages a greater understanding of one another and feelings. And our feelings, as Audre Lorde wrote, "are our most genuine paths to knowledge" (Lorde, 2004, p. 91).

Pedagogy

We know participants bring different skill sets and styles to the classroom. All Teach This Poem lessons create an environment in which participants can encounter poems through several entry points that begin with shared experiences. As a pedagogy that attempts to foster poetic sensibility while recognizing the importance of different perspectives, communities, and ways of learning, each lesson in the *Teach This Poem* book follows the same general trajectory:

- A warm-up related to the chosen poem that helps focus participants for the rest of the lesson.

- Careful noticing of a related resource from another genre or academic discipline. This gives participants an alternate entry point to the poem, as well as practice with noticing visual details.
- Using skills practiced with the related resource, an individual silent reading of the poem while creating a record of words, phrases, and poetic structures that stand out. This helps participants begin to think about what might be important in the poem, and provides a list of ideas they may be able to use as evidence in later discussions and writing.
- Oral readings of the poem, either by the poet in a video or two different participants. Listening participants add what they hear in the poem to what they saw on the page. This provides more ideas for evidence.
- Pair shares or small group discussions that give everyone a chance to speak and help participants who are uncomfortable speaking in a large group generate ideas. This adds more voices to large group discussions.
- A large group synthesis based on what participants have noticed in the poem and the related resource, guided by questions to open up multiple interpretations.
- Optional extension activities.

The lessons that appear each week are generally targeted toward upper-middle and lower-high school students. They include questions and brief activity suggestions that teachers can incorporate in the framework above.

We also recognize that public school teachers, the primary audience for *Teach This Poem*, need to integrate this pedagogy with their state's standards and the fundamentals of the art form. To assist with this integration, at a minimum all the lessons in *Teach This Poem* satisfy a generally accepted English/Language Arts Standard that includes identifying details, a poetic glossary term, and additional curricular context.

It is our intention that educators tailor the lessons we provide to their participants' grade levels and needs. Above all, we encourage educators to use their own creativity as they adapt *Teach This Poem*, as only they can, for the specific participants they teach.

Book Rationale

As mentioned earlier, poetry can become a unique and powerful way to address a range of subjects with young people. We believe that by engaging with poems and developing a poetic sensibility, young people will be better prepared to meet the challenges and opportunities they will face as they become citizens of the world.

Many of the lessons in this volume have been published online in Teach This Poem during the first six years of the series. In that form, they responded to the events of the time, established celebrations and holidays, and more generally, adhered to the education standards that continue to develop. Most of those lessons have been updated for this collection.

As of September 2023, nearly 40,000 educators received poems and accompanying lessons through Teach this Poem. Many have asked that we organize a group into a book for quick reference. The result is *Teach This Poem: Volume I, The Natural World*. The poems are categorized around the sub-themes of "Why Poetry?" and "The Natural World: Future, Present, and Past."

1 Why Poetry?

Introduction

In his pivotal essay "How to Read a Poem," Academy of American Poets Chancellor Emeritus Edward Hirsch writes:

> Literature is, and has always been, the sharing of experience, the pooling of human understanding about living, loving, and dying. Successful poems welcome you in, revealing ideas that may not have been foremost in the writer's mind in the moment of composition. The best poetry has a magical quality—a sense of being more than the sum of its parts—and even when it's impossible to articulate this sense, this something more, the power of the poem is left undiminished.

Poets from all walks of life have always had a knack for writing about the importance, value, and nuance of poetry in original and mind-opening ways. That is where the lesson plans in *Teach this Poem: Volume 1, The Natural World* begin. In her brief poem "There is no frigate like a book (1263)," Emily Dickinson considers literature's ability to carry the reader to faraway places; students encounter this poem alongside a watercolor of a ship at sea from the Metropolitan Museum and discuss how they feel when they are engrossed in a story. Layli Long Soldier, while seemingly writing about the role of gesture in showing what is genuine, relates this to what happens in poems. This chapter also includes lesson plans around poems by June Jordan, Alberto Ríos, and Walt Whitman, among others.

"These Poems"
by June Jordan

These poems
they are things that I do
in the dark
reaching for you
whoever you are
and
are you ready?

These words
they are stones in the water
running away

These skeletal lines
they are desperate arms for my longing and love.

I am a stranger
learning to worship the strangers
around me

whoever you are
whoever I may become.

Related Resource

Water and stones in the Black Sea.

George Chernilevsky, *Black sea water near Fiolent*, 2009. Photograph, Wikimedia Commons.

Why Poetry?

Activities

1. **Warm-up**: Look closely at the image of underwater stones. Write down what you notice in the photograph.
2. **Before Reading the Poem**: Imagine and write down what stones might do in this setting (for example, sing), even if it's not physically possible. With a partner, take turns sharing what you noticed and imagined.
3. **Reading the Poem**: Silently read "These Poems" by June Jordan. What do you notice about the poem? Note any words, phrases, or poetic structures that stand out to you and any questions you might have.
4. **Listening to the Poem**: Enlist two volunteers and listen as the poem is read aloud twice. What did you hear that you did not previously notice when you were reading the poem? Write down any additional words and phrases that stood out to you.
5. **Small Group Discussion**: This may be a good time to review the term metaphor. Take turns sharing what you noticed in the poem with a small group. What is similar or different about your observations? Identify any metaphors you noticed.
6. **Large Group Discussion**: What do you think the speaker in the poem might be saying about her poems? What evidence in the poem leads you to think this?
7. **Extension for Grades 7–8**: Write a poem or paragraph using the idea of stones and what you imagined they could do. Try to use metaphors in your writing.
8. **Extension for Grades 9–12**: Look closely at the last two stanzas of the poem. Read more information about June Jordan in the More Context section. How do you think these stanzas might have applied to her life? How do these stanzas apply to your life? Write an essay about your ideas.

More Context

From the Archive: June Jordan's 1978 Postcard

In this 1978 postcard from our archive, June Jordan writes a short statement about herself to Kathy Engel, the Academy of American Poets' program associate at the time. Jordan, who had recently published her collection *Things That I Do in the Dark: Selected Poetry* (Random House, 1977) shortly before the date of this postcard, was in discussion with Engel regarding a few Academy-sponsored events. The previous month, Engel had confirmed Jordan's participation in a library project in Connecticut; she was scheduled to present readings and workshops at the Bridgeport Public Library and the Danbury Public Library that May. This statement was likely meant to be included as part of the introductions or promotional materials for these events. Here you can read the postcard where Jordan identifies herself not just as a poet, but also as a person interested in engaging with poetry as a political act.

Glossary Term

Metaphor a comparison between essentially unlike things or the application of a name or description to something to which it is not literally applicable.

Why Poetry?

"There is no frigate like a book (1263)"
by Emily Dickinson

There is no Frigate like a Book
To take us Lands away,
Nor any Coursers like a Page
Of prancing Poetry –
This Traverse may the poorest take
Without oppress of Toll –
How frugal is the Chariot
That bears a Human soul.

Related Resource

Sailing ship on stormy waters.

Albert Ernest Markes, *Ship at sea*, late 19th century. Watercolor, Metropolitan Museum of Art.

Activities

1. **Warm-up:** Think of one or two words you associate with a ship at sea. Share them with a partner and continue sharing with a small group of people.
2. **Before Reading the Poem:** Look closely at the watercolor *Ship at Sea*. Write down what you notice about how the ship was painted—colors, brush strokes, etc. What impressions do you have of this ship? Use what you noticed to provide evidence. Talk with a partner about your impressions.
3. **Reading the Poem:** Silently read "There is no frigate like a book (1263)" by Emily Dickinson. What do you notice about the poem? Note any words, phrases, or poetic structures that stand out to you and any questions you might have.

4. **Listening to the Poem**: Enlist two volunteers and listen as the poem is read aloud twice. What did you hear that you did not previously notice when you were reading the poem? Write down any additional words and phrases that stood out to you.
5. **Small Group Discussion**: Take turns sharing what you noticed in the poem with a small group. Based on the details you just shared and your activities from the beginning of this lesson, why do you think Emily Dickinson compared reading a book to a frigate?
6. **Large Group Discussion**: What do you think this poem might be saying about books and poetry? What similes and metaphors does Dickinson use in this poem to make you think this way?
7. **Extension for Grades 7–8**: How do you feel when you are really engrossed in a book, story, or poem? What similes and/or metaphors would you use if you were going to write about how you feel? Write a paragraph that lists these similes and metaphors and explain why you chose them.
8. **Extension for Grades 9–12**: Read some other poems by Emily Dickinson and choose two that interest you. Write a script for a presentation on these poems that highlights any comparisons, punctuation, or poetic structures that you think might be important. Read your script to several people.

More Context
Discussing Emily Dickinson's Work

What does it feel like to read a Dickinson poem? What is your sense of her musicality, sound, rhythm, and use of space? Do you read these poems quickly or slowly? What do you think about the capitalization and punctuation? Find or develop more discussion questions about Emily Dickinson's work to share with your group.

Glossary Term

Enjambment the continuation of a sentence or clause across one poetic line break.

"From WHEREAS ["WHEREAS when offered..."]"
by Layli Long Soldier

WHEREAS when offered an apology I watch each movement the shoulders
high or folding, tilt of the head both eyes down or straight through
me, I listen for cracks in knuckles or in the word choice, what is it
that I want? To *feel* and mind you I feel from the senses—I read
each muscle, I ask the strength of the gesture to move like a poem.
Expectation's a terse arm-fold, a failing noun-thing
I scold myself in the mirror for holding.

Because I learn from young poets. One sends me new work spotted
with salt crystals she metaphors as her tears. I feel her phrases,
"I say," and "Understand me," and "I wonder."

Pages are cavernous places, white at entrance, black in absorption.
Echo.

If I'm transformed by language, I am often
crouched in footnote or blazing in title.
Where in the body do I begin;

Related Resource

Woman with children.

Dorothea Lange, *Migrant mother*, 1936. Photograph, Library of Congress.

Activities

1. **Warm-up**: Gather with a partner and take turns making a gesture with your upper body that shows a strong feeling. What emotion does your partner's gesture suggest to you and why?
2. **Before Reading the Poem**: What details do you notice in the photograph by Dorothea Lange? How are the people in the photograph positioned? What can you learn from the positions of their bodies and the expression on the woman's face? With a partner, take turns sharing what you've noticed and learned.
3. **Reading the Poem**: Silently read "from WHEREAS ['WHEREAS when offered…']" by Layli Long Soldier. What do you notice about the poem? Note any words, phrases, or poetic structures that stand out to you and any questions you might have.
4. **Listening to the Poem**: Enlist two volunteers and listen as the poem is read aloud twice. What did you hear that you did not previously notice when you were reading the poem? Write down any additional words and phrases that stood out to you.
5. **Small Group Discussion**: What words, phrases, and poetic structures did you notice in the poem? How does the poem relate to the warm-up activity and to the photograph? What do you notice about the poem's structure?
6. **Large Group Discussion**: What do you think the poem is saying about the importance of body language? In what context is the poem's speaker noticing someone's body language? Do you think this is important or unimportant? Why?
7. **Extension for Grades 7–8**: In your small group, create a tableau staging either a genuine or pretend apology. Keep the reason for the apology you're working on a secret from other groups. Take turns presenting your tableaux to everyone. As each group presents, share the details you notice and your thoughts about what the apology might be for.
8. **Extension for Grades 9–12**: Read the joint resolution from the More Context section below. What word do you notice repeated throughout the apology? Review the definition of the word whereas if you're not familiar with the different uses of this word. How does this apology inform your reading of Layli Long Soldier's poem, which is the beginning of a longer series?

More Context

Document

Joint Resolution 14, introduced on April 30, 2009 and passed by the Senate of the United States during the 111th Congress, opens with the following statement: "To acknowledge a long history of official depredations and ill-conceived policies by the Federal Government regarding Indian tribes and offer an apology to all Native Peoples on behalf of the United States." Read more of the joint resolution that inspired Layli Long Soldier's poetry collection *Whereas*.

Glossary Term

Poetic diction the language, including word choice and syntax, that sets poetry apart from other forms of writing.

Chapter 1

"Poetry"
by Marianne Moore

I too, dislike it: there are things that are important beyond all this fiddle.
  Reading it, however, with a perfect contempt for it, one discovers that there is in
it after all, a place for the genuine.
    Hands that can grasp, eyes
    that can dilate, hair that can rise
      if it must, these things are important not because a

high-sounding interpretation can be put upon them but because they are
  useful; when they become so derivative as to become unintelligible, the
same thing may be said for all of us—that we
  do not admire what
  we cannot understand. The bat,
    holding on upside down or in quest of something to

eat, elephants pushing, a wild horse taking a roll, a tireless wolf under a tree, the immovable critic twinkling his skin like a horse that feels a flea, the base—
ball fan, the statistician—case after case
  could be cited did
  one wish it; nor is it valid
    to discriminate against "business documents and

school-books"; all these phenomena are important. One must make a distinction
  however: when dragged into prominence by half poets, the result is not poetry,
nor till the autocrats among us can be
  "literalists of
  the imagination"—above
    insolence and triviality and can present

for inspection, imaginary gardens with real toads in them, shall we have
  it. In the meantime, if you demand on the one hand, in defiance of their opinion—
the raw material of poetry in
  all its rawness, and
  that which is on the other hand,
    genuine, then you are interested in poetry.

Related Resources

Temple garden in Kyoto, Japan.

Wikimedia Commons contributor, Garden of a temple at Myoshinji, Kyoto, Japan, 2020. Photograph, Wikimedia Commons.

Common toad.

George Chernilevsky, *Bufo bufo*, 2015. Photograph, Wikimedia Commons.

Activities

1. **Warm-up**: Look at the image of the garden for several minutes and write down all the words that would help someone imagine the garden in their mind's eye. Similarly, look at the image of the common toad and write down all the details you can about what this toad looks like.
2. **Before Reading the Poem**: Using the details you collected, write four lines that place your toad in an imaginary garden.

3. **Reading the Poem**: Silently read "Poetry" by Marianne Moore. What do you notice about the poem? Note any words, phrases, or poetic structures that stand out to you and any questions you might have.
4. **Listening to the Poem**: Enlist two volunteers and listen as the poem is read aloud twice. What did you hear that you did not previously notice when you were reading the poem? Write down any additional words and phrases that stood out to you.
5. **Small Group Discussion**: What do you think Marianne Moore might mean by "imaginary gardens with real toads in them"? Use your thoughts from the activities at the beginning of this lesson to help you.
6. **Large Group Discussion**: What do you think Marianne Moore might think about poetry? What role might she think poetry plays in life? Make sure you use evidence from your reading of the poem and your writings to support your answers.
7. **Extension for Grades 7–8**: Using what you've learned in this lesson, play a type of verbal charades in which you try to get someone to figure out what animal you are thinking about by using detailed words to describe it.

8. **Extension for Grades 9–12**: Read "The Jelly Fish" by Marianne Moore. What words does she use to describe a real jellyfish in imaginary water? Write a short poem in which you describe a real animal that inspires you in an imaginary environment, so that others will feel the same way you do. Take turns sharing your poems.

More Context
Essay

In her essay "The Marianne Moore of First Intention," Heather Cass White says, "The best-known example of Moore's ruthless self-editing is what she did to her poem 'Poetry.' When she first published it in 1919, 'Poetry' was a thirty-line poem divided into five delicately rhymed, neatly syllabic stanzas. In 1925, she published it as 13 lines of free verse. In 1932, she published it as three stanzas of rhymed syllabics. Finally, in 1967's *Complete Poems*, it appears, in its entirety, as three lines. Three lines!" Read more of White's essay about Marianne Moore's poetry and her approach to editing poetry.

Glossary Term

Ars poetica a poem that explores the art of poetry by examining the role of the poet and their relationship to the poem and the act of writing.

"Valentine for Ernest Mann"
by Naomi Shihab Nye

You can't order a poem like you order a taco.
Walk up to the counter, say, "I'll take two"
and expect it to be handed back to you
on a shiny plate.

Still, I like your spirit.
Anyone who says, "Here's my address,
write me a poem," deserves something in reply.
So I'll tell a secret instead:
poems hide. In the bottoms of our shoes,
they are sleeping. They are the shadows
drifting across our ceilings the moment
before we wake up. What we have to do
is live in a way that lets us find them.

Once I knew a man who gave his wife
two skunks for a valentine.
He couldn't understand why she was crying.
"I thought they had such beautiful eyes."
And he was serious. He was a serious man
who lived in a serious way. Nothing was ugly
just because the world said so. He really
liked those skunks. So, he re-invented them
as valentines and they became beautiful.
At least, to him. And the poems that had been hiding
in the eyes of skunks for centuries
crawled out and curled up at his feet.

Maybe if we re-invent whatever our lives give us
we find poems. Check your garage, the odd sock
in your drawer, the person you almost like, but not quite.
And let me know.

Related Resource

Skunk about to spray.

Wallace Keck, *Skunk about to spray*, 2011. Photograph, Wikimedia Commons.

Activities

1. **Warm-up**: Look closely at the image of the skunk for several minutes. Write a detailed description of what you see, and in particular anything you find beautiful about this animal.
2. **Before Reading the Poem**: Read your description to another person. The person listening should tell you whether or not they felt the beauty of the skunk from the description, and offer suggestions to help you describe its beauty. Make sure both people have a chance to be readers and responders.
3. **Reading the Poem**: Silently read "Valentine for Ernest Mann" by Naomi Shihab Nye. What do you notice about the poem? Note any words, phrases, or poetic structures that stand out to you and any questions you might have.
4. **Listening to the Poem**: Watch and listen carefully to Naomi Shihab Nye as she reads her poem. What did you hear that you did not previously notice when you were reading the poem? Write down the words, phrases, and poetic structures she emphasizes, if any. Add any additional words and phrases that stood out to you.
5. **Small Group Discussion**: Take turns sharing what you noticed in a small group. How do these things make the skunk beautiful? What might the speaker in the poem mean when she says, "the poems that had been hiding / in the eyes of skunks for centuries / crawled

out and curled up at his feet"? What "crawled out and curled up at [your] feet" when you looked at the photo of the skunk?
6. **Large Group Discussion**: What might the speaker in the poem mean when she says, "Maybe if we re-invent whatever our lives give us / we find poems"?
7. **Extension for Grades 7–8**: Find an item that you don't think is particularly beautiful. Bring it to class and look at it for a long while. Reinvent the object with a detailed description of that item in a poem.
8. **Extension for Grades 9–12**: Look carefully at an item you have at home that you don't think is particularly beautiful. Try to reinvent the item the way the husband reinvented the eyes of the skunks. Do you agree that "Maybe if we reinvent whatever our lives give us / we find poems"? Write a letter to Naomi Shihab Nye telling her what you think and why.

More Context

Video

In a discussion on inspiration, Naomi Shihab Nye says, "And I do think that sometimes one of the most precious elements of affinity and inspiration is gathering up poems so that you'll be able to put your fingers on them later to hand to someone at the appropriate moment, to give to the friend who needs it right then, to email to the person who's hurting." Watch the video or read the transcript of the discussion.

Glossary Term

Stanza a group of lines that form the basic unit of a poem.

"Bracken"
by Kai Carlson-Wee

Don't go in search of the perfect word.
Don't go looking for signs of redemption,
the purified water of gods. The language
will enter your mouth when it needs to.
The beauty will find you. The meaning
will come. Don't go smiling. Don't go
certain of one true voice. Go ambiguous,
lonely, disguised in the basic math. Take
nothing for granted. Escape what you are,
what you wish you will one day become.
It doesn't matter. The skin dies. The worm
lives a whole year in darkness. The clouds
go on rising away from the falling rain.
Even the good love inside you will vanish.
The wheels will seize and the trickling stream
at the top of the mountain will carve out
a valley below. The world will give you
an opening always. The night sky. The moon
lifting over the tall and mysterious pines.
Hold out the feather you found last night
in the bracken. All it can offer is already
there in your hand.

Related Resource

House sparrow tail feathers.

Wikimedia Commons contributor, *Feather growth bars*, 2010. Photograph, Wikimedia Commons.

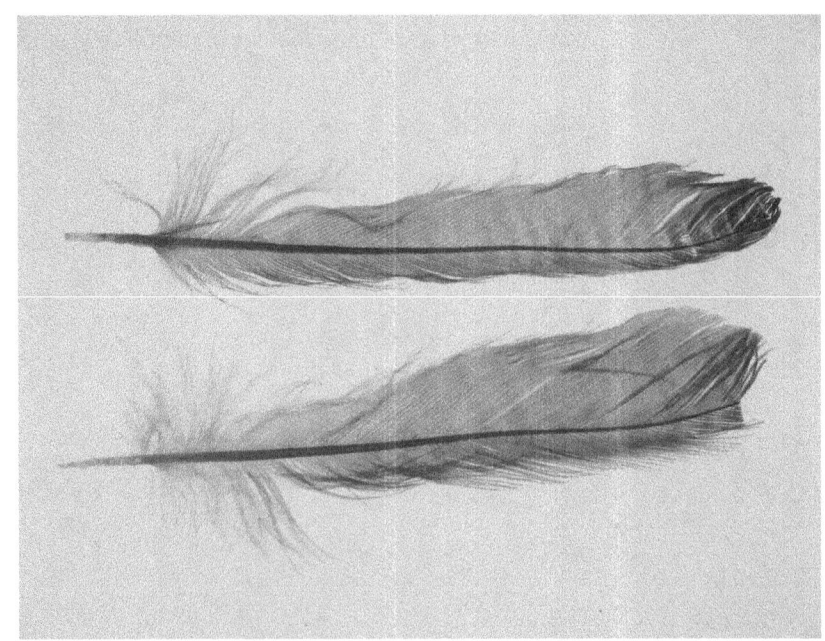

Activities

1. **Warm-up**: On a clean sheet of paper, quickly draw what you can remember of a feather. The drawing doesn't have to perfectly depict a feather—instead, focus on experiencing the way your hand moves as you draw rapidly. When you have finished, write a few sentences describing your image and how drawing this feather felt.
2. **Before Reading the Poem**: Look very closely at this image of two feathers. Add details to your drawing based on what you notice, then add more to your written description based on these new details. If your feelings about the image have changed over the course of this exercise, be sure to include this in your writing. Take turns sharing your drawing and your sentences with a partner.
3. **Reading the Poem**: Silently read "Bracken" by Kai Carlson-Wee. What do you notice about the poem? Note any words, phrases, or poetic structures that stand out to you and any questions you might have. What do you think bracken means?
4. **Listening to the Poem**: Enlist two volunteers and listen as the poem is read aloud twice. What did you hear that you did not previously notice when you were reading the poem? Write down any additional words and phrases that stood out to you.
5. **Small Group Discussion**: With a partner and two other people, take turns sharing the words, phrases, and poetic structures you noticed. What might these tell you about what the speaker in the poem thinks about the process of writing?
6. **Large Group Discussion**: How do you think the art of drawing compares with the art of writing a poem? Do you think the last three lines of the poem can apply to drawing as well? What is the same? What is different?
7. **Extension for Grades 7–8**: Take or find a photograph of an object from nature that interests you. Look carefully at the photograph and write a detailed poem or paragraph that evokes how you feel about it.
8. **Extension for Grades 9–12**: How do you imagine a scientist might describe a feather? How might a poet describe one? Write an essay that shows what you think the different descriptions would be like. What could we learn from reading both?

More Context

Poems

Find more poems about paintings, sculptures, and other forms of visual art, as well as poems about artists and the artistic process on Poets.org.

Glossary Term

Nocturne a poem set at night.

"On Gathering Artists"
by Alberto Ríos

> *Who does a job well, and very well—*
> *These are the artists, those curious*
> *Lights.*

We are cobblers of the song
And barkers of the carnival word,
We are tailors of the light
And framers of the earth.
We fish among the elements
And hunt the elusive green in gray and blue.
We drink forbidden waters
And eat an invisible food.

In this time of electronic-mail and facsimile
Conversation, we send as our voice
The poem, the bridge, the circuit, the cure
Whose electricity is made from dreams,
Whose song is sung in the colors yet unnamed
Drawn from the solitary études of the soul
And given up in tender to the world.

How easy to spend a day writing a poem,
How hard to spend a life writing a thousand.
A poem, a bridge, a story, a circuit,
Cures, laws, bowls—
The warp and weave and waft of iron
And paper and light and salt:
We labor for a lifetime
But take every day off.
Who knows what to make of us?

We are not the ribcage, but the legs;
We are not the steering wheel, but the headlamps.
We gather happily, if not often. We can't
Sit still. We hurry off. Good-bye to us,
Hello to us, a tip of the hat
To us, as we go about
The drumming of our stars.

Related Resource

Circuit board.

jpramirez, *Untitled*. Illustration, Adobe.

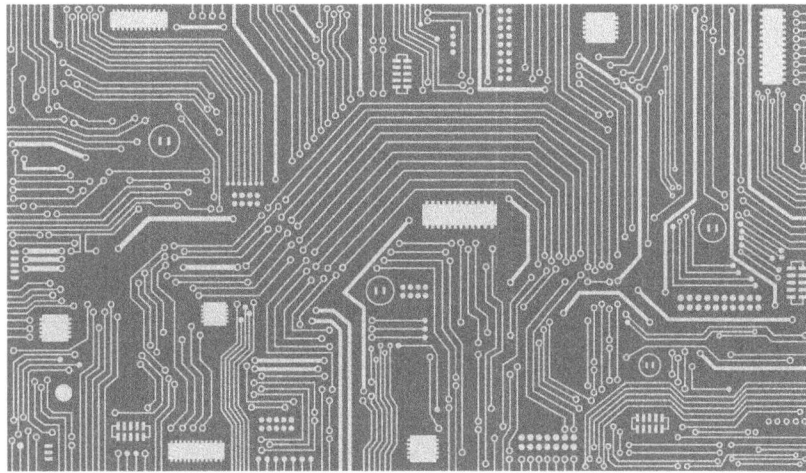

Activities

1. **Warm-up**: What are some ways artists contribute to society? Ask a few people you know, and write down what they say.
2. **Before Reading the Poem**: Look very closely at the image of the circuit board. Make a list of the details you see, including any lines, connections, or shapes. What is your overall impression of the image? Take turns sharing the details you noticed with a partner.
3. **Reading the Poem**: Silently read "On Gathering Artists" by Alberto Ríos. What do you notice about the poem? Note any words, phrases, or poetic structures that stand out to you and any questions you might have.
4. **Listening to the Poem**: Enlist two volunteers and listen as the poem is read aloud twice. What did you hear that you did not previously notice when you were reading the poem? Write down any additional words and phrases that stood out to you.
5. **Small Group Discussion**: Take turns sharing the words, phrases, and poetic structures you noticed in a small group. What might these tell you about what the speaker in the poem thinks about poets and other artists?
6. **Large Group Discussion**: How are artists "barkers of the carnival world," "tailors of the light," and "framers of the earth"? How might they "fish among the elements"? Think back to the image of a circuit board. How might a poem be "the circuit, the cure / Whose electricity is made from dreams"? Why are these metaphors important to the narrative of the poem?
7. **Extension for Grades 7–8**: Think about a car: How might a poet be "not the steering wheel, but the headlamps"? Write a few paragraphs that illustrate your ideas. Include a metaphor that shows what you think a poet or artist might be like.

8. **Extension for Grades 9–12**: What are some similarities and differences between a circuit board and a poem? What does the poem tell us that the image of the circuit board cannot? Do you think a circuit board is a good metaphor for a poem? Write an essay that discusses these questions.

More Context

Essay

In "Some Thoughts on the Integrity of the Single Line in Poetry," Alberto Ríos writes in praise of "lines that are long in their moment, that make me linger and give me the effect of having encountered something, something worth stopping for—the antithesis of our times, which seem to be all about getting somewhere else, and fast, and we're late already."

Glossary Term

Line a fundamental unit in verse that carries meaning horizontally across the page and vertically from one line to the next.

"The Indications [excerpt]"
by Walt Whitman

The words of the true poems give you more than poems,
They give you to form for yourself, poems, religions, politics, war, peace, behavior, histories essays, romances, and everything else,
They balance ranks, colors, races, creeds, and the sexes,
They do not seek beauty—they are sought,
Forever touching them, or close upon them, follows beauty, longing, fain, love-sick.

They prepare for death—yet are they not the finish, but rather the outset,
They bring none to his or her terminus, or to be content and full;
Whom they take, they take into space, to behold the birth of stars, to learn one of the meanings,
To launch off with absolute faith—to sweep through the ceaseless rings, and never be quiet again.

Related Resource

Stellar nursery photographed by the Hubble telescope.

NASA, ESA and A. Nota (STScI/ESA), *Hubble's exquisite view of a stellar nursery*, 2005. Image, nasa.gov.

Activities

1. **Warm-up**: Look closely at the image of a stellar nursery taken by the Hubble Telescope, in which infant stars are forming within a nebula. Look at it for several moments, then write down the specific details you noticed.

2. **Before Reading the Poem**: Find a partner and talk about the details you see. How do these details come together as a whole? How does the whole make you feel?
3. **Reading the Poem**: Silently read "The Indications [excerpt]" by Walt Whitman. What do you notice about the poem? Note any words, phrases, or poetic structures that stand out to you and any questions you might have.
4. **Listening to the Poem**: Enlist two volunteers and listen as the poem is read aloud twice. What did you hear that you did not previously notice when you were reading the poem? Write down any additional words and phrases that stood out to you.
5. **Small Group Discussion**: With members of a small group, take turns sharing what you noticed. What do you think the speaker in the poem might be saying about what poems do? How might they make him feel?
6. **Large Group Discussion**: How did looking at the image of the birth of stars prepare you to think about how the poem's speaker feels about poetry?
7. **Extension for Grades 7–8**: How do you feel about poetry? What images can you think of to evoke this feeling? Draw one of these images and include the words and feelings this image evokes.
8. **Extension for Grades 9–12**: Read the article "NASA's James Webb Telescope shows many stars in Southern Ring Nebula," look carefully at the two images at the end of the article, and pick one. What words would you use to describe the nebula in the photo you chose? What emotions does it evoke in you? Write a paragraph that includes your description and how it makes you feel. Write another paragraph about how your description differs from NASA's. Why might both kinds of descriptions be important?

More Context
Essay

In his essay "The Ceaseless Rings of Walt Whitman," Langston Hughes writes about Whitman's life and his poetry stating, "Certainly, his poems contain us all. The reader cannot help but see his own better self therein."

Glossary Term

End-stopped line a metrical line that contains a complete phrase or sentence, or a poetic line that ends with punctuation.

"A Way of Seeing"
by Kwame Dawes

It all comes from this dark dirt,
memory as casual as a laborer.

Remembrances of ancestors
kept in trinkets, tiny remains

that would madden anthropologists
with their namelessness.

No records, just smells of stories
passing through most tenuous links,

trusting in the birthing of seed from seed;
this calabash bowl of Great-grand

Martha, born a slave's child;
this bundle of socks, unused

thick woolen things for the snow—
he died, Uncle Felix, before the ship

pushed off the Kingston wharf,
nosing for winter, for London.

He never used the socks, just
had them buried with him.

So, sometimes forgetting the panorama
these poems focus like a tunnel,

to a way of seeing time past,
a way of seeing the dead.

Related Resources

Valley and mountain range in Pakistan.

Zeeshan Ali Qadri, *View of valley and mountain range in Northern Pakistan*, 2016. Photograph, Wikimedia Commons.

Mountains through a tunnel in Pakistan.

Wikimedia Commons contributor, *View from a newly built tunnel on Karakoram Highway, Gilgit-Baltistan*, 2015. Photograph, Wikimedia Commons.

Activities

1. **Warm-up**: Think of something you or your family might have, or might have talked about, that belonged to one of your ancestors. Why do you think this item may be important to members of your family? Is it important to you? Why or why not? If you cannot think of anything, imagine something that might be important to you and/or your family. Taking turns, share this information with a partner.
2. **Before Reading the Poem**: Look closely at the two photographs. Write down what you notice in each one. How are they similar to each other? How are they different? Write down your thoughts.
3. **Reading the Poem**: Silently read "A Way of Seeing" by Kwame Dawes. What do you notice about the poem? Note any words, phrases, or poetic structures that stand out to you and any questions you might have.
4. **Listening to the Poem**: Enlist two volunteers and listen as the poem is read aloud twice. What did you hear that you did not previously notice when you were reading the poem? Write down any additional words and phrases that stood out to you.
5. **Small Group Discussion**: Take turns sharing what you noticed in the poem with a small group. How might what you noticed relate to the two photographs you looked at earlier? Discuss how you think the photographs were taken, as well as the content of the photographs.
6. **Large Group Discussion**: What items in the poem seemed to be important to the speaker? Why do you think these items were important? What might this have to do with the way the photographs you looked at earlier were taken?

7. **Extension for Grades 7–8**: If possible, bring in a photograph of the object that belonged to one of your ancestors or of something that is important to your family today. If you are imagining the object, make a detailed drawing of what you imagined. Prepare a presentation about why this object was important to your ancestor or is important to your present family, and to you; or prepare a presentation about why a present-day object is important to your family and to you. Give this presentation to a small group of people you know.
8. **Extension for Grades 9–12**: Read the essay "Kinship of Clay" by Joseph Drew Lanham. What did you learn? What might the speaker of the poem experience by looking at and holding the calabash bowl that belonged to Great-grand Martha? Why do you think Uncle Felix had the woolen socks buried with him? Why does this poem "focus like a tunnel / to a way of seeing time past / a way of seeing the dead"? Write an essay that answers these questions using evidence from the poem and your discussion of the photographs.

More Context

Poems

Read more poems about family by poets such as Richard Blanco, Nikki Giovanni, Yesenia Montilla, and more.

Glossary Term

Imagery language in a poem that represents a sensory experience.

2 The Natural World

Introduction

The climate crisis is one of the most important issues facing today's youth. In a 2022 interview with the Academy of American Poets, B. K. Fischer, first poet laureate of Westchester County, said:

> poems are acts of attention—they can wake us up to the here and now. Eco-poetry and eco-writing can ground us in the conditions of the place where we are, uncovering layers of local history, human ecologies, and natural ecologies. […] [P]oetry invites us to ask "Where am I?" with as much particularity as poetry has always devoted to the question "Who am I?" Answering the question "Where am I?" changes the scale, broadens perspective, and deepens recognition of our place in ecosystems, local and global.

This chapter includes poems that address the changing natural world from a number of perspectives. In an epistolary poem, Matthew Olzmann addresses climate crisis–related extinctions through a letter written to someone in the future; students engage with a 1902 French lithograph from the Library of Congress and write their own poems or letters to the future. In a poem about spring, the 24th United States Poet Laureate Ada Limón considers survival and celebration; alongside it, students learn about the myth of the phoenix and consider Limón's use of the leafing tree as metaphor. In a rhyming poem, 19th-century Muskogee Creek poet Alexander Posey laments the coyote's shrinking habitat as white settlers advance; students encounter the poem alongside a photograph of a coyote and discuss how the tone of the poem shifts. This section also includes lesson plans around poems by Arthur Sze, Linda Hogan, William Carlos Williams, and more.

Part 1: Future

"Letter to Someone Living Fifty Years From Now"
by Matthew Olzmann

Most likely, you think we hated the elephant,
the golden toad, the thylacine and all variations
of whale harpooned or hacked into extinction.

It must seem like we sought to leave you nothing
but benzene, mercury, the stomachs
of seagulls rippled with jet fuel and plastic.

You probably doubt that we were capable of joy,
but I assure you we were.

We still had the night sky back then,
and like our ancestors, we admired
its illuminated doodles
of scorpion outlines and upside-down ladles.

Absolutely, there were some forests left!
Absolutely, we still had some lakes!

I'm saying, it wasn't all lead paint and sulfur dioxide.
There were bees back then, and they pollinated
a euphoria of flowers so we might
contemplate the great mysteries and finally ask,
"Hey guys, what's transcendence?"

And then all the bees were dead.

Part 1

Related Resource

Futuristic depiction of 2000 from the early 20th century.

Albert Robida, *Le Sortie de l'opéra en l'an 2000*, ca. 1902. Hand-colored lithograph, Library of Congress.

Activities

1. **Warm-up**: Sketch a picture of what you think the world will look like in 50 years. With a partner, take turns describing what you sketched.
2. **Before Reading the Poem**: Look at the lithograph *Leaving the Opera in the Year 2000*. With a partner, discuss how this image from 1902 compares to your sketch.
3. **Reading the Poem**: Silently read "Letter to Someone Living Fifty Years From Now" by Matthew Olzmann. What do you notice about the poem? Note any words, phrases, or poetic structures that stand out to you and any questions you might have.
4. **Listening to the Poem**: Enlist two volunteers and listen as the poem is read aloud twice. What did you hear that you did not previously notice when you were reading the poem? Write down any additional words and phrases that stood out to you.
5. **Small Group Discussion**: Take turns sharing what you noticed in the poem with a small group, and call back the lines you think are important by saying them aloud with a partner. Based on these details, how might the poem compare or contrast with your image of the future or the lithograph *Leaving the Opera in the Year 2000*?
6. **Large Group Discussion**: What imagery stands out in the poem? Why? If you don't know the definition of imagery, refer to the glossary. What might the speaker in the poem want the future person to know about the past?
7. **Extension for Grades 7–8**: Write a poem to someone 50 years in the future. What do you want to tell this person about your life right now? Or, with a small group, discuss ways to make your school or neighborhood more environmentally friendly. Share

your ideas in a large group discussion. To help you, research information about any green initiative your school or community might have.
8. **Extension for Grades 9–12**: Create a time capsule. With a small group of people, decide what you want to include and when you want to open it.

More Context

Article

Poetry can serve as a tool for addressing concerns about the changing world and climate, as well as provide words of guidance about the future, moving forward, and new beginnings. Find more poems and activities that contemplate and offer solutions for the future, and create an additional writing prompt about Olzmann's poem.

Glossary Term

Epistolary poem a poem of direct address that reads as a letter, also known as an epistle.

"Characteristics of Life"
by Camille T. Dungy

> *A fifth of animals without backbones could be at risk of extinction, say scientists.*
>
> —BBC Nature News

Ask me if I speak for the snail and I will tell you
I speak for the snail.
         speak of underneathedness
and the welcome of mosses,
         of life that springs up,
little lives that pull back and wait for a moment.

I speak for the damselfly, water skeet, mollusk,
the caterpillar, the beetle, the spider, the ant.
         I speak
from the time before spinelessness was frowned upon.

Ask me if I speak for the moon jelly. I will tell you
         one thing today and another tomorrow
and I will be as consistent as anything alive
on this earth.

         I move as the currents move, with the breezes.
What part of your nature drives you? You, in your cubicle
ought to understand me. I filter and filter and filter all day.

Ask me if I speak for the nautilus and I will be silent
as the nautilus shell on a shelf. I can be beautiful
and useless if that's all you know to ask of me.

Ask me what I know of longing and I will speak of distances
      between meadows of night-blooming flowers.
         I will speak
the impossible hope of the firefly.

         You with the candle
burning and only one chair at your table must understand
   such wordless desire.

         To say it is mindless is missing the point.

Related Resource

Garden snail.

Frederick P. Nodder, *The garden snail*, 1789. Illustration, *The Naturalist's Miscellany Vol. 1* (Nodder & Co., 1789–1813).

Activities

1. **Warm-up**: Look closely at this image of snails. What do you notice about them? Look again. What else do you see? You might also want to gather pictures of all of the animals listed in the poem and think about what these animals might have in common.
2. **Before Reading the Poem**: Read the epigraph that accompanies the poem. Read this short article about invertebrates. Discuss with a partner or small group what might make invertebrates more at risk for extinction.
3. **Reading the Poem**: Silently read "Characteristics of Life" by Camille T. Dungy. What do you notice about the poem? Note any words, phrases, or poetic structures that stand out to you and any questions you might have.
4. **Listening to the Poem**: Enlist two volunteers and listen as the poem is read aloud twice. What did you hear that you did not previously notice when you were reading the poem? Write down any additional words and phrases that stood out to you.
5. **Small Group Discussion**: Take turns sharing what you noticed in the poem with a small group. Based on the details you just shared and your activities from the beginning of class, what can you tell about the speaker? What part of the speaker's nature seems to drive them? What part of your nature drives you and why?
6. **Large Group Discussion**: How does the epigraph relate to the poem? How might the poem be different without it? Why might the speaker feel the need to "speak for" these creatures? What is the impact of the title on the poem?
7. **Extension for Grades 7–8**: Imagine a conversation between two or more of the quieter creatures in the poem. For example, what might the damselfly say to the caterpillar? How might these animals discuss extinction?

8. **Extension for Grades 9–12**: Research biodiversity in your community, city, or state. Write a poem that answers the question: What part of your nature drives you? What kinds of creatures might you want to "speak for"?

More Context

Interview

Read this interview where Camille T. Dungy says:

> There are a lot of things we have in common despite the personal and collective histories that also give us our particular sets of experiences. I am as interested in the commonalities as I am in the ways we use those commonalities differently. This is true with humans as it is with nonhuman life. I am interested in commonality and all the potential commonality can breed. To speak up for the life forms of the world in this sort of radically empathetic way is, as you suggest, a kind of witness. It's also a kind of activism. And it's also a kind of love.

Glossary Term

Speaker the voice of a poem, similar to a narrator in fiction.

"The Everglades"
by Campbell McGrath

Green and blue and white, it is a flag
for Florida stitched by hungry ibises.

It is a paradise of flocks, a cornucopia
of wind and grass and dark, slow waters.

Turtles bask in the last tatters of afternoon,
frogs perfect their symphony at dusk—

in its solitude we remember ourselves,
dimly, as creatures of mud and starlight.

Clouds and savannahs and horizons,
its emptiness is an antidote, its ink

illuminates the manuscript of the heart.
It is not ours though it is ours

to destroy or preserve, this the kingdom
of otter, kingfisher, alligator, heron.

If the sacred is a river within us, let it flow
like this, serene and magnificent, forever.

Related Resource

Watch the video "On the Trail: Everglades National Park."

Crocodile in Everglades National Park.

Conor Knighton, "On the Trail: Everglades National Park," 2016. Screenshot from video, *CBS Sunday Morning*.

Activities

1. **Warm-up**: Before reading the poem, watch the video "On the Trail: Everglades National Park." Then write down what you remember.

2. **Before Reading the Poem**: What did you learn from this video? Taking turns, share what you learned with another person. How do you feel about the Everglades after watching the video?
3. **Reading the Poem**: Silently read "The Everglades" by Campbell McGrath. What do you notice about the poem? Note any words, phrases, or poetic structures that stand out to you and any questions you might have.
4. **Listening to the Poem**: Enlist two volunteers and listen as the poem is read aloud twice. What did you hear that you did not previously notice when you were reading the poem? Write down any additional words and phrases that stood out to you.
5. **Small Group Discussion**: In a small group, take turns sharing what you noticed in the poem. What did you learn from the poem? How do you feel about the Everglades after reading and hearing this poem? Provide evidence from the poem to support your answers.
6. **Large Group Discussion**: What do you remember from watching the video? What do you remember from the poem? How is the language in the poem different from that in the video? What do you think is the function of these different types of language?
7. **Extension for Grades 7–8**: Think about one plant and one animal that live in the Everglades. Imagine that the plant and animal are having a conversation about how they relate to each other's lives and how they are similar to and different from each other. Write down this conversation.
8. **Extension for Grades 9–12**: Conduct research on the changes that are occurring in the Everglades because of climate change. Write an essay that describes one of the changes and its effects. What might be done to adapt to this change or to stop this change from happening? Present your findings.

More Context

Article

In "10 Public Lands with Powerful Native American Connections," the U.S. Department of the Interior acknowledges that:

> one of the several tribes connected to the Everglades National Park region in Florida is the Seminole Tribe of Florida…Eventually, more than 3,000 Seminoles were forcibly removed from their lands on their own prolonged Trail of Tears. However, a few hundred Seminoles hid in the Everglades and never signed a peace treaty. Today, their descendants remain in the region, part of the Seminole Tribe of Florida, the Miccosukee Tribe of Florida and some unofficial Seminole tribes.

Glossary Term

Pastoral a creative tradition, as well as individual work idealizing rural life and landscapes.

"The Shapes of Leaves"
by Arthur Sze

Ginkgo, cottonwood, pin oak, sweet gum, tulip tree:
our emotions resemble leaves and alive
to their shapes we are nourished.

Have you felt the expanse and contours of grief
along the edges of a big Norway maple?
Have you winced at the orange flare

searing the curves of a curling dogwood?
I have seen from the air logged islands,
each with a network of branching gravel roads,

and felt a moment of pure anger, aspen gold.
I have seen sandhill cranes moving in an open field,
a single white whooping crane in the flock.

And I have traveled along the contours
of leaves that have no name. Here
where the air is wet and the light is cool,

I feel what others are thinking and do not speak,
I know pleasure in the veins of a sugar maple,
I am living at the edge of a new leaf.

Related Resource

Clear-cutting in the Blue Ridge Mountains.

Tennessee Valley Authority, *Bad Lands, Unaka National Forest, Southern Appalachians*, 1936. Photograph, Wikimedia Commons.

Activities

1. **Warm-up**: When the trees in your area are in full leaf, find a tree that speaks to you. In writing, describe the details of that tree and why you are attracted to it. Pay particular attention to the tree's leaves. You may even want to draw a picture of a leaf you particularly like.
2. **Before Reading the Poem**: Look at the image of clear-cutting. Write down the details you see. How does this image make you feel? Look up the definition of clear-cutting if you don't know what it means. With a partner, discuss how you feel about clear-cutting after seeing the image.
3. **Reading the Poem**: Silently read "The Shapes of Leaves" by Arthur Sze. What do you notice about the poem? Note any words, phrases, or poetic structures that stand out to you and any questions you might have.
4. **Listening to the Poem**: Enlist two volunteers and listen as the poem is read aloud twice. What did you hear that you did not previously notice when you were reading the poem? Write down any additional words and phrases that stood out to you.
5. **Small Group Discussion**: With a small group, research the types of trees and birds mentioned in the poem. Take turns sharing what you learned with members of your group.
6. **Large Group Discussion**: Based on the activities and what you have learned, what do you think the speaker of the poem might be saying about how different leaves and trees make him feel? What is happening to some of these trees? What do you think it might mean to be "living at the edge of a new leaf"?
7. **Extension for Grades 7–8**: Based on the warm-up activity, write a poem that shows how you feel about the tree you chose. Use the details you wrote down to help a reader understand how you feel and why that tree spoke to you. Imagine what the tree said to you and include it in your poem.
8. **Extension for Grades 9–12**: Who or what are "the others" the speaker references in the last stanza? What might they be thinking? If you could speak for them, what would they say? Read the definition of personification in the glossary, and write a poem from the perspective of one of the trees in "The Shapes of Leaves."

More Context

Article

"Leaves make food for the tree, and this tells us much about their shapes. For example, the narrow needles of a Douglas fir can expose as much as three acres of chlorophyll surface to the sun." Read more about what leaves do and the full anatomy of a tree in the Forest Services' "Anatomy of a tree."

Glossary Term

Tone a literary device that conveys the author's attitude toward the subject, speaker, or audience of a poem.

"The Forest for the Trees"
by Rena Priest

I have seen a tree split in two
from the weight of its opposing branches.
It can survive, though its heart is exposed.
I have seen a country do this too.

I have heard an elder say
that we must be like the willow—
bend not to break.
I have made peace this way.

My neighbors clear-cut their trees,
leaving mine defenseless. The arborist
says they'll fall in the first strong wind.
Together we stand. I see this now.

I have seen a tree grown around
a bicycle, a street sign, and a chainsaw,
absorbing them like ingredients
in a great melting pot.

When we speak, whether or not
we agree, the trees will turn
the breath of our words
from carbon dioxide into air—

give us new breath
for new words,
new chances to listen,
new chances to be heard.

Related Resource

Watch the video "How Trees Secretly Talk to Each Other in the Forest."

Trees in a forest.

Produced by Laura Leadmon, "How Trees Secretly Talk to Each Other in the Forest | Decoder." Screenshot from video, National Geographic.

Activities

1. **Warm-up**: Read the definition of an idiom provided below. Work with your classmates to generate a list of idioms that you know or create your own idioms. After you've developed your class list, read over the entire list. What do you notice about idioms?
2. **Before Reading the Poem**: Watch the video "How Trees Secretly Talk to Each Other in the Forest." What did you learn about trees? In what ways are they important?
3. **Reading the Poem**: Silently read "The Forest for the Trees" by Rena Priest. What do you notice about the poem? Note any words, phrases, or poetic structures that stand out to you and any questions you might have.
4. **Listening to the Poem**: Enlist two volunteers and listen as the poem is read aloud twice. What did you hear that you did not previously notice when you were reading the poem? Write down any additional words and phrases that stood out to you.
5. **Small Group Discussion**: Taking turns, share what you noticed about the poem with a small group. Based on the details you just shared with your small group and the video from the beginning of these activities, how does the speaker feel about nature and its relationship to humans? What do you make of the first stanza: "I have seen a tree split in two / from the weight of its opposing branches. / It can survive, though its heart is exposed. / I have seen a country do this too"?
6. **Large Group Discussion**: What do you think of the title? Have you ever heard of the idiom cannot see the forest for the trees? If so, how does this idiom compare to the poem and to the idioms that the group generated?
7. **Extension for Grades 7–8**: Think back to the video that you watched. What might a tree language sound like? What do you think trees would say to each other? Write a poem that explores these ideas or your own ideas about nature.
8. **Extension for Grades 9–12**: Using the idioms from the first activity, research the history of your idiom(s), if available. Write a creative response, such as a poem, or an analytical response about your chosen idiom(s).

More Context

Interview

November 2022 Poem-a-Day Guest Editor Jake Skeets said about the connection between land and poetry, "Land is both resistance and reflection, and we understand land as landscape, nature, wilderness in the American consciousness. However, land takes shape and form in many different ways where I come from." Read the full interview.

Glossary Term

Idiom a short expression peculiar to a language, people, or place that conveys a figurative meaning without a literal interpretation of the words used in the phrase.

"Dead Stars"
by Ada Limón

Out here, there's a bowing even the trees are doing.
    Winter's icy hand at the back of all of us.
Black bark, slick yellow leaves, a kind of stillness that feels
so mute it's almost in another year.

I am a hearth of spiders these days: a nest of trying.

We point out the stars that make Orion as we take out
    the trash, the rolling containers a song of suburban thunder.

It's almost romantic as we adjust the waxy blue
    recycling bin until you say, *Man, we should really learn
some new constellations*.

And it's true. We keep forgetting about Antlia, Centaurus,
    Draco, Lacerta, Hydra, Lyra, Lynx.

But mostly we're forgetting we're dead stars too, my mouth is full
    of dust and I wish to reclaim the rising—

to lean in the spotlight of streetlight with you, toward
    what's larger within us, toward how we were born.

Look, we are not unspectacular things.
    We've come this far, survived this much. What

would happen if we decided to survive more? To love harder?

What if we stood up with our synapses and flesh and said, *No*.
    No, to the rising tides.

Stood for the many mute mouths of the sea, of the land?

What would happen if we used our bodies to bargain

for the safety of others, for earth,
    if we declared a clean night, if we stopped being terrified,

if we launched our demands into the sky, made ourselves so big
people could point to us with the arrows they make in their minds,

rolling their trash bins out, after all of this is over?

Part 1

Related Resource

The constellation Orion.

Wikimedia Commons contributor, *Orion*, 2004. Photograph, Wikimedia Commons.

Activities

1. **Warm-up**: With a partner, take turns sharing one or two associations that come to your mind when you think of looking at the night sky.
2. **Before Reading the Poem**: Look at the image of the constellation Orion and write down what you notice (patterns of brightness and darkness, the placement of the stars, etc.). Does this image remind you of anything? How does it make you feel?
3. **Reading the Poem**: Silently read "Dead Stars" by Ada Limón. What do you notice about the poem? Note any words, phrases, or poetic structures that stand out to you and any questions you might have.
4. **Listening to the Poem**: Enlist two volunteers and listen as the poem is read aloud twice. What did you hear that you did not previously notice when you were reading the poem? Write down any additional words and phrases that stood out to you.
5. **Small Group Discussion**: Take turns sharing the words, phrases, and poetic structures that you noticed with a small group. Develop a composite list to share with others. One person from your group should write down your composite list to share in the large group discussion.
6. **Large Group Discussion**: Do you see any repetitions or patterns in the collection of words, phrases, and poetic structures? What

might these repetitions or patterns tell you? At what point in the poem does the speaker start asking questions? What are these questions about? What does the word "this" in the last line of the poem refer to? What is your evidence?
7. **Extension for Grades 7–8**: Write an illustrated essay about doing something that would make you "so big / people could point to [you] with the arrows they make in their minds."
8. **Extension for Grades 9–12**: Research more about star formation and evolution. Why do you think the title of the poem is "Dead Stars"? What are the dead stars in the poem? What is the speaker comparing herself to when she says, "my mouth is full / of dust and I wish to reclaim the rising"? Write a personal essay or poem that indicates what you would do to help promote "the safety of others" or the rebirth of the earth.

More Context

Interview

In an interview filmed in 2010, Ada Limón speaks about the relationship between poetry and noticing. She says:

> We find it hard to settle our brains down, and poetry offers us that silence, that quiet space, and allows us to reconnect with ourselves, or with an idea, or with an emotion.... It's almost as if the poets are offering a religion of noticing things, or a religion of paying attention, and it's nice that it doesn't have any connotation other than that. Just notice. Just pay attention. Just be here.

Watch the video.

Glossary Term

Lyric poetry non-narrative poetry that expresses the speaker's emotions and feelings, often with songlike qualities.

"Radium Dream"
by Sheila Black

We come at the wrong time of year by a hair
or a week, and the brown birds flying onward,
out of reach. My son tilts his head. A minor star-
burst of cranes lights the far corner of
the sky—stragglers, fewer than expected,
but enough to glitter the air with strangeness—
these birds with their necks not tucked in, forming
their odd cries. When they land by the shore,
their toothpick legs appear hardly enough
to hold up their robust bodies. Often

I think—"That's not really happening is it?" as though I
were acting in a film or a vision of a life. On the
highway, they warn us not to drink—too much
uranium, leached down from the abandoned mines.
The cranes twist their necks to stab the quick-
light of fish. Do cranes know how to
swim? And why is swimming so different than flying?

Now, aloft again, they apparate with uncanny
quickness into cloud. How does the eye lose
them—is it how high they rise? The bones

in my son's hand, they tell me, have stopped growing
too early. They act like this is a problem, but I
have radium dreams—a brightness: Him, me, you, the
cranes, and in them nothing dies.

Related Resource

Watch the National Geographic video of sandhill cranes, and look closely at an interactive periodic table.

Cranes taking flight.

Produced by Amy Rankin, "Thousands of Cranes Take Flight in One of Earth's Last Great Migrations | National Geographic." Screenshot from video, National Geographic.

Activities

1. **Warm-up**: Watch the National Geographic video of sandhill cranes. In a few words, write down what you noticed and your reaction to it. What did you observe about these birds?
2. **Before Reading the Poem**: Look closely at this interactive periodic table. Find and click on radium, and read the description. What do you notice about this element? Look again. What else do you notice?
3. **Reading the Poem**: Silently read "Radium Dream" by Sheila Black. What do you notice about the poem? Note any words, phrases, or poetic structures that stand out to you and any questions you might have.
4. **Listening to the Poem**: Enlist two volunteers and listen as the poem is read aloud twice. What did you hear that you did not previously notice when you were reading the poem? Write down any additional words and phrases that stood out to you.
5. **Small Group Discussion**: Take turns sharing what you noticed in the poem with a small group. Based on the details you just shared with your small group and your discussions from the earlier activities, what is unique about the mother and son's bird-watching experience? What imagery in the poem stands out to you?
6. **Large Group Discussion**: Why do you think the poem is titled "Radium Dream"? Think back to what you learned about radium before you read the poem. What does radium relate to in the poem? What is the tone at the end of the poem? What is the speaker's wish?
7. **Extension for Grades 7–8**: How might the cranes feel about being watched? Think about what you saw in the video and write a poem from the perspective of the cranes. Or find a song, photograph, or piece of art that feels like it could be in conversation with this poem. Share your findings.

8. **Extension for Grades 9–12**: Read about the radium girls hired during the 1920s to paint the numbers onto watch faces and write a research paper about Mae Keane, a radium girl who lived to be 107 years old.

More Context
Article

For the 13th edition (1926) of the *Encyclopædia Britannica*, Marie Curie, co-winner of the 1903 Nobel Prize for Physics and winner of the 1911 Nobel Prize for Chemistry, wrote the entry on radium with her daughter Irène Curie, later Irène Joliot-Curie and co-winner of the 1935 Nobel Prize for Chemistry.

Read this article from *Encyclopædia Britannica* to learn more about this radioactive metal and how it was discovered.

Glossary Term

Free verse poetry that isn't dictated by an established form or meter, often influenced by the rhythms of speech.

"Nimbawaadaan Akiing / I Dream a World"
by Margaret Noodin

Nimbawaadaan akiing
I dream a world

atemagag biinaagami
of clean water

gete-mitigoog
ancient trees

gaye gwekaanimad
and changing winds.

Nimbawaadaan akiing
I dream a world

izhi-mikwendamang
of ones who remember

nandagikenindamang gaye
who seek the truth and

maamwidebwe'endamang waabang
believe in tomorrow together.

Nimbawaadaan akiing
I dream a world

izhi-biimiskobideg giizhigong
where our path in the sky

waabandamang naasaab
can be seen as clearly as

gaa-izhi-niibawid wiijibemaadizid
the place where our neighbor once stood.

Related Resource

Listen to the song "Meet Me By the Water" by Brenda MacIntyre.

Northern California redwood trees.

Carol M. Highsmith, *Northern California redwoods*, 2012. Photograph, Library of Congress.

Activities

1. **Warm-up**: Finish this sentence: "I dream a world..." What do you dream for the world? If you feel comfortable, share with a partner.
2. **Before Reading the Poem**: Listen to the song "Meet Me By the Water" by Brenda MacIntyre. What does the song make you think about? How does the song make you feel?
3. **Reading the Poem**: Silently read "Nimbawaadaan Akiing / I Dream a World" by Margaret Noodin. What do you notice about the poem? Note any words, phrases, or poetic structures that stand out to you and any questions you might have.
4. **Listening to the Poem**: Enlist two volunteers and listen as the poem is read aloud twice. What did you hear that you did not previously notice when you were reading the poem? Write down any additional words and phrases that stood out to you.
5. **Small Group Discussion**: Take turns sharing what you noticed in the poem with a small group of people. Based on the details you just shared with your small group and the earlier activities, what does the speaker envision for the future? How does it compare to your vision and the song?
6. **Large Group Discussion**: How does the repetition of the line "I dream a world" impact your reading of the poem? How might the poem be different without it? Read the poet's About the Poem statement:

   > This poem was written after hearing Kwame Alexander and Rachel Martin talk about Martin Luther King, Jr.'s speech "I Have a Dream" which was inspired by Langston Hughes' poem "I Dream a World." With all we've lost and learned this past year, and all that remains to be repaired, I thought perhaps we should all sit down and dream harder and more often with more clarity and infinite diversity.

   What does this statement make you think about?
7. **Extension for Grades 7–8**: Think back to your sentence from the first activity. Continue to expand on your vision for a future world. What do you want that world to include? Create a piece of art (poem, song, collage, photograph, etc.) that embodies your vision and share it with others.

8. **Extension for Grades 9–12**: Alone or with a small group, read more poems by Native American poets. Choose three or more poets and create a group anthology.

More Context
Article

"The Ojibwe language has historically been repressed by policymakers and educators in the U.S. and Canada, though there are many, complex reasons why fewer people today speak Ojibwe." Read more about Ojibwe, and explore the variety of dialects of this endangered language with The Ojibwe People's Dictionary, a searchable, talking Ojibwe-English dictionary that features the voices of Ojibwe speakers.

Glossary Term

Couplet a two-line stanza, or two successive lines of verse, rhymed or unrhymed.

Part 2: Present

"In Praise of Okra"
by January Gill O'Neil

No one believes in you
like I do. I sit you down on the table
& they overlook you for
fried chicken & grits,
crab cakes & hush puppies,
black-eyed peas & succotash
& sweet potatoes & watermelon.

Your stringy, slippery texture
reminds them of the creature
from the movie *Aliens*.

But I tell my friends if they don't like you
they are cheating themselves;
you were brought from Africa
as seeds, hidden in the ears and hair
of slaves.

Nothing was wasted in our kitchens.
We took the unused & the throwaways
& made feasts;
we taught our children
how to survive,
adapt.

So I write this poem
in praise of okra
& the cooks who understood
how to make something out of nothing.
Your fibrous skin
melts in my mouth—
green flecks of flavor,
still tough, unbruised,
part of the fabric of earth.
Soul food.

Related Resource

Read the *Encyclopædia Britannica* entry on okra.

Okra.

Wikimedia Commons contributor, *Oklahoma-grown okra*, 2021. Photograph, Wikimedia Commons.

Activities

1. **Warm-up**: Name a food or dish associated with your region, culture, heritage, or family that you really like.
2. **Before Reading the Poem**: Read the *Encyclopædia Britannica* entry on okra, and write down any words and phrases that catch your eye. What did you learn from this entry?
3. **Reading the Poem**: Silently read "In Praise of Okra" by January Gill O'Neil. What do you notice about the poem? Note any words, phrases, or poetic structures that stand out to you and any questions you might have.
4. **Listening to the Poem**: Enlist two volunteers and listen as the poem is read aloud twice. What did you hear that you did not previously notice when you were reading the poem? Write down any additional words and phrases that stood out to you.
5. **Small Group Discussion**: Take turns sharing the notes you've taken with the rest of your small group. What do these words, phrases, and poetic structures suggest about the importance of okra to the poem's speaker? How did the entry from the encyclopedia help you understand this poem?
6. **Large Group Discussion**: Why does the speaker in the poem think her friends are "cheating themselves" if they don't like okra? What evidence in the poem leads you to this conclusion?
7. **Extension for Grades 7–8**: Think about the food that you named during the warm-up. Do you know why it is important in your

region, culture, heritage, or family? What is its history? If you don't know the answers to these questions, think instead about why you like this particular food. Write a poem or essay that describes what you know about this food and why it is different from other foods you eat. Remember to use descriptive words.

8. **Extension for Grades 9–12**: Research the phrase "soul food." How does the phrase influence your understanding of this poem? With this in mind, what do you think okra might symbolize for the speaker? Why do you think the speaker has chosen to end the poem with "soul food?"

More Context

Article

Writing about Lucille Clifton's poem "won't you celebrate with me," the poet Safiya Sinclair says, "What a balm and a blessing this poem has been to me. I have carried this sonnet—both an ode to the self and also an act of resistance—inside me like gospel, like armor." Read notes from Sinclair and 11 other contemporary poets about what poems they recommend reading during Black History Month and why.

Glossary Term

Praise poem a poem of tribute or gratitude.

"Remember"
by Joy Harjo

Remember the sky that you were born under,
know each of the star's stories.
Remember the moon, know who she is.
Remember the sun's birth at dawn, that is the
strongest point of time. Remember sundown
and the giving away to night.
Remember your birth, how your mother struggled
to give you form and breath. You are evidence of
her life, and her mother's, and hers.
Remember your father. He is your life, also.
Remember the earth whose skin you are:
red earth, black earth, yellow earth, white earth
brown earth, we are earth.
Remember the plants, trees, animal life who all have their
tribes, their families, their histories, too. Talk to them,
listen to them. They are alive poems.
Remember the wind. Remember her voice. She knows the
origin of this universe.
Remember you are all people and all people
are you.
Remember you are this universe and this
universe is you.
Remember all is in motion, is growing, is you.
Remember language comes from this.
Remember the dance language is, that life is.
Remember.

Related Resource

Sunset at a mountain lake.

Madeleine Fuchs Holzer, *The sunset at Lake Chelan in the Cascade Mountains*, 2019. Photograph, private collection.

Activities

1. **Warm-up**: With a partner, take turns making a gesture with your hands that shows how you are feeling right now. Take turns sharing a few words that describe your feelings.
2. **Before Reading the Poem**: Look carefully at the photograph of the sunset at Lake Chelan in the Cascade Mountains. Take notes on what you see. How does this photograph make you feel? Note the details in the photo that make you feel this way. Is this a scene you would like to remember? Why or why not?
3. **Reading the Poem**: Silently read "Remember" by Joy Harjo. What do you notice about the poem? Note any words, phrases, or poetic structures that stand out to you and any questions you might have.
4. **Listening to the Poem**: Enlist two volunteers and listen as the poem is read aloud twice. What did you hear that you did not previously notice when you were reading the poem? Write down any additional words and phrases that stood out to you.
5. **Small Group Discussion**: Take turns sharing your notes on the poem in a small group. Focus on the words, phrases, and poetic structures that stood out to you. What do they tell you about what is important to the speaker in the poem? Give specific examples as you discuss this. Does the feeling or tone in the poem relate to the feeling or tone in the photo that you looked at earlier? How?
6. **Large Group Discussion**: Based on your reading of the poem, how do you think the speaker in the poem feels about the connectedness of all things? Provide evidence from the poem to back up your ideas.
7. **Extension for Grades 7–8**: Think about the line from the poem, "all is in motion, is growing, is you." Write your own poem that shows how this line fits who you are. Start as many lines as you can with the same word, the way Harjo does in "Remember." Pick a word you think would be important to the meaning of your poem.
8. **Extension for Grades 9–12**: Think about the line from the poem, "Remember the dance language is, that life is." How are both language and life a dance? Write a poem about life in which language dances on the page. You can read about concrete poems in the glossary, or think about how to use multimedia to present your poem.

More Context

Interview

Joy Harjo says in an interview with the Academy of American Poets:

> I keep thinking of a Poetry Ancestor Tree... How would you construct that? I always tell my students about poetry ancestors. Every poem has so many poetry ancestors. How can we construct a poetry ancestor map of America that would include and start off with poetry of indigenous nations? Those strands would

continue into the present with the wonderful young Native poets we have right now. I guess what strikes me is the diversity—the diversity of Native poetry, which was here and is here and is still growing, and the diversity of American poetry, which has roots all over the world—and I've always wanted to show that, ultimately, there's a root system that's connected all over the Americas, which is one body and all over the world. A healthy ecosystem is a system of diversity. That's the same thing in poetry, different poetry streams.

Read more of Harjo's words in "An Interview with Joy Harjo, U.S. Poet Laureate."

Glossary Term

Anaphora a poetic technique in which successive phrases or lines begin with the same words, often resembling a litany.

"The Tree Sparrows"
by Joseph O. Legaspi

We suffer through blinding equatorial heat,
refusing to unfold the suspended bamboo shade
nested by a pair of hardworking, cheerless sparrows.
We've watched them fly in-and-out of their double
entryways, dried grass, twigs clamped in their beaks.
They skip, nestle in their woodsy tunnel punctured
with light, we presume, not total darkness, their eggs
aglow like lunar orbs. What is a home? How easily
it can be destroyed: the untying of traditional ropes,
pull, the scroll-unraveling. For want of a sweltering
living room to be thrown into relief by shadow.

The sunning couple perch open-winged, tube lofty
as in Aristophanes' city of birds, home made sturdy
by creature logic and faith that it will all remain afloat.

Related Resource

Wooden birdhouse.

Unknown photographer, *Untitled*, 2017. Photograph, Pxhere.

Activities

1. **Warm-up**: Gather a cardboard paper towel or gift wrap roll, three small boxes (no more than 12 by 18 inches), scissors, and tape or glue.
2. **Before Reading the Poem**: Take 20 minutes to build a birdhouse using the materials you have. Make it as sturdy and long-lasting as possible.

3. **Reading the Poem**: Silently read "The Tree Sparrows" by Joseph O. Legaspi. What do you notice about the poem? Note any words, phrases, and poetic structures that stand out to you and any questions you might have.
4. **Listening to the Poem**: Enlist two volunteers and listen as the poem is read aloud twice. What did you hear that you did not previously notice when you were reading the poem? Write down any additional words and phrases that stood out to you.
5. **Small Group Discussion**: Share your birdhouse with a small group along with a description of the process you used and how you felt about it. What characteristics do your birdhouses and processes have in common?
6. **Large Group Discussion**: How did the members of your group feel as they were trying to build sturdy birdhouses? How sturdy were your birdhouses? Citing evidence from the poem, what does Legaspi say is necessary to make a home sturdy? Based on your building experience, do you agree or disagree?
7. **Extension for Grades 7–8**: Write down the step-by-step instructions you used to build your birdhouse so that someone else could create an identical birdhouse. Highlight the things you did to make it especially sturdy.
8. **Extension for Grades 9–12**: The speaker of the poem asks, "What is a home?" Do you think the poem answers that question? If so, how? What do you think makes a home? List the characteristics that make a home, including emotional and material things. Write a list poem from your notes. If you aren't familiar with the list poetry form, read the definition in the glossary.

More Context

Article

What is a home? Writer and editor Julie Beck explores the topic in *The Atlantic* article "The Psychology of Home: Why Where You Live Means So Much." Beck opens with the following statement: "There's a reason why the first thing we often ask someone when we meet them, right after we learn their name, is 'Where's home for you?'"

Glossary Term

Allusion a reference to a person, event, or literary work.

"A Small Needful Fact"
by Ross Gay

Is that Eric Garner worked
for some time for the Parks and Rec.
Horticultural Department, which means,
perhaps, that with his very large hands,
perhaps, in all likelihood,
he put gently into the earth
some plants which, most likely,
some of them, in all likelihood,
continue to grow, continue
to do what such plants do, like house
and feed small and necessary creatures,
like being pleasant to touch and smell,
like converting sunlight
into food, like making it easier
for us to breathe.

Related Resource

Rabbit in a garden.

Carol M. Highsmith, *A semipermanent resident of the garden at the Buffalo Bill Center of the West...*, 2015. Photograph, Library of Congress.

Activities

1. **Warm-up**: Look closely at the image of the rabbit in the garden. What do you notice in the photograph? How does it make you feel? What associations do you have with a rabbit in a garden? Write down your answers to these questions.

2. **Before Reading the Poem**: Talk with a partner about your answers using the notes you have written down. Make sure both of you get a chance to speak.
3. **Reading the Poem**: Silently read "A Small Needful Fact" by Ross Gay. What do you notice about the poem? Note any words, phrases, or poetic structures that stand out to you and any questions you might have.
4. **Listening to the Poem**: Enlist two volunteers and listen as the poem is read aloud twice. What did you hear that you did not previously notice when you were reading the poem? Write down any additional words and phrases that stood out to you.
5. **Small Group Discussion**: What words, phrases, and poetic structures does Ross Gay repeat in the poem? Why do you think he repeats them?
6. **Large Group Discussion**: How does your reaction to the photograph of the rabbit help you understand the poem? Why does the poet end with breathing? What do you think the poem is saying about Eric Garner? What is your evidence?
7. **Extension for Grades 7–8**: With a small group, gather paper cups, a small bag of potting soil, and flower seeds. Following the directions on the packet of seeds, plant the seeds in the cups. Place the cups in a sunny place and give them the right amount of water. Once sprouted, plant the seedlings in a community garden, a pot, or a garden of your own. Keep a journal of how you care for your plants. What stands out to you about what you have to do to keep the plants alive?
8. **Extension for Grades 9–12**: What does a gardener do? Why do you think the poet uses the image of Eric Garner's role as a gardener? What is he trying to tell us about Eric Garner's personality? Read several of the newspaper articles that were written about the death of Eric Garner. Based on evidence from this poem and on evidence from the articles, write an essay about what you think happened the day of Eric Garner's death and how you feel about it.

More Context

Article

Read "Beyond the Chokehold: The Path to Eric Garner's Death" by Al Baker, J. David Goodman, and Benjamin Mueller featured in *The New York Times* to learn more about Eric Garner's life and the events that occurred on July 17, 2014 that resulted in his homicide.

Glossary Term

Repetition   the poetic technique of repeating the same word or phrase multiple times within a poem.

"In cold spring air"
by Reginald Gibbons

In cold
      spring air the
white wisp-
      visible
breath of
      a blackbird
singing—
      we don't know
to un-
      wrap these blind-
folds we
      keep thinking
we are
      seeing through

Related Resource

Watch the video of Paul McCartney singing "Blackbird."

Paul McCartney singing "Blackbird."

Paul McCartney Catalog, "Blackbird (Live Version f[r]om 70s)," posted December 30, 2009. Screenshot from video, YouTube.

Activities

1. **Warm-up**: Think about a cold day during the beginning of spring, and write a quick sentence about how that day makes you feel.
2. **Before Reading the Poem**: Watch the video of Paul McCartney singing "Blackbird." Note what stands out to you in the lyrics. With a partner, discuss what you've written about the song, any particular lyrics you were drawn to, and how the song might relate to a cold day in spring.

3. **Reading the Poem**: Silently read "In cold spring air" by Reginald Gibbons. What do you notice about the poem? Note any words, phrases, or poetic structures that stand out to you and any questions you might have.
4. **Listening to the Poem**: Enlist two volunteers and listen as the poem is read aloud twice. What did you hear that you did not previously notice when you were reading the poem? Write down any additional words and phrases that stood out to you.
5. **Small Group Discussion**: In a small group, share what you noticed that seemed important or unusual in this poem.
6. **Large Group Discussion**: What is the poem saying to you? What evidence do you have to support this? What do you notice about the lines in the poem and the number of syllables in each line? What do you think this structure adds to the poem, if anything?
7. **Extension for Grades 7–8**: How does it feel to be in cold spring air? Write a five-line poem that uses five syllables per line and describes how you feel. Use strong, descriptive words to show your feelings, but do not tell the reader directly that you feel cold.
8. **Extension for Grades 9–12**: Due to climate change, the weather each season is in flux. Write an essay describing what spring used to be like where you live and how it has changed. What, if anything, is your community doing to adapt to these changes? How do you think your community should respond? Discuss your thoughts with a small group.

More Context

Article

> The growing seasons are shifting. Spring is arriving earlier, winters are shorter, and the number of freezing days is declining. These changes affect the timing of many life cycle events, such as when flowers bloom or when pollinators emerge. Changes in the timing of these events can have adverse effects on ecosystems, because different species may respond to different environmental cues, resulting in a misalignment between species that may rely on one another.

Read more to learn about how the seasons are affected by changes in our climate in "How Climate Change May Affect Winter 'Weather Whiplash.'"

Glossary Term

Syllabic verse a poetic form that has a fixed or constrained number of syllables per line as well as per stanza.

"Cherry Blossoms"
by Toi Derricotte

I went down to
mingle my breath
with the breath
of the cherry blossoms.

There were photographers:
Mothers arranging their
children against
gnarled old trees;
a couple, hugging,
asks a passerby
to snap them
like that,
so that their love
will always be caught
between two friendships:
ours & the friendship
of the cherry trees.

Oh Cherry,
why can't my poems
be as beautiful?

A young woman in a fur-trimmed
coat sets a card table
with linens, candles,
a picnic basket & wine.
A father tips
a boy's wheelchair back
so he can gaze
up at a branched
heaven.

    All around us
the blossoms
flurry down
whispering,

   Be patient
you have an ancient beauty.
                 Be patient,
           you have an ancient beauty.

Related Resource

Silk scrolls with cherry blossoms.

Hirose Kain, *Cherry blossoms*, 19th century. Color on silk, Wikimedia Commons.

Activities

1. **Warm-up**: Quickly write down a list of any associations you have with the phrase "ancient beauty." Try not to edit yourself during this exercise; focus instead on writing whatever comes to mind. When you have finished, pare your list down to two or three associations and share them with a partner.
2. **Before Reading the Poem**: Look very closely at the image of the hanging scrolls from 19th-century Japan. Write down what you see when you look at the image from a distance and close up. What descriptive words capture the essence of the cherry blossoms in this image? Share what you have noticed with a partner.
3. **Reading the Poem**: Silently read "Cherry Blossoms" by Toi Derricotte. What do you notice about the poem? Note any words, phrases, or poetic structures that stand out to you and any questions you might have.
4. **Listening to the Poem**: Enlist two volunteers and listen as the poem is read aloud twice. What did you hear that you did not previously notice when you were reading the poem? Write down any additional words and phrases that stood out to you.
5. **Small Group Discussion**: Take turns sharing the words, phrases, and poetic structures that you noticed in the poem with a small group. How do these words, phrases, and poetic structures relate to the cherry blossoms on the scrolls, if at all?

6. **Large Group Discussion**: How do you think the speaker in the poem feels about the cherry blossoms she sees? What is your evidence? What does the speaker in the poem compare the cherry tree and its blossoms to? Think back to the warm-up and the image of the scrolls. What thoughts might the speaker in the poem have about "ancient beauty"?
7. **Extension Grades 7–8**: Write a paragraph or a poem about something that you think has "an ancient beauty." Be sure to use adjectives, similes, and metaphors to help the reader understand the unique beauty of this object.
8. **Extension for Grades 9–12**: What is the symbolism of cherry blossoms, or *sakura*, in Japanese culture? What can you learn about the introduction of these trees to the United States? Conduct research to find out the answers to these questions, then write an essay telling the story of the trees. Include your thoughts about the importance of these trees.

More Context

Essay

In her essay "The Bond of Living Things: Poems of Ancestry," Toi Derricotte writes, "In the end, our connection to the past is more than a personal connection; it places us within a lifeline that extends before and beyond us, it places and holds us between the wings of something vast and eternal." Read this essay to find out more about what Derricotte thinks about ancestry.

Glossary Term

Personification the attribution of human qualities to animals, inanimate objects, or abstract ideas.

"Map"
by Linda Hogan

This is the world
so vast and lonely
without end, with mountains
named for men
who brought hunger
from other lands,
and fear
of the thick, dark forest of trees
that held each other up,
knowing fire dreamed of swallowing them
and spoke an older tongue,
and the tongue of the nation of wolves
was the wind around them.
Even ice was not silent.
It cried its broken self
back to warmth.
But they called it
ice, wolf, forest of sticks,
as if words would make it something
they could hold in gloved hands,
open, plot a way
and follow.

This is the map of the forsaken world.
This is the world without end
where forests have been cut away from their trees.
These are the lines wolf could not pass over.
This is what I know from science:
that a grain of dust dwells at the center
of every flake of snow,
that ice can have its way with land,
that wolves live inside a circle
of their own beginning.
This is what I know from blood:
the first language is not our own.

There are names each thing has for itself,
and beneath us the other order already moves.
It is burning.
It is dreaming.
It is waking up.

Related Resources

Visit the NASA webpage "Ice Shelf Collapse in East Antarctica" to view the images of the ice shelf, and view a map of Native American Land.

Before and after images of an ice shelf collapse in Antarctica.

NASA, *Ice shelf collapse in east Antarctica*, 2022. Images, NASA.

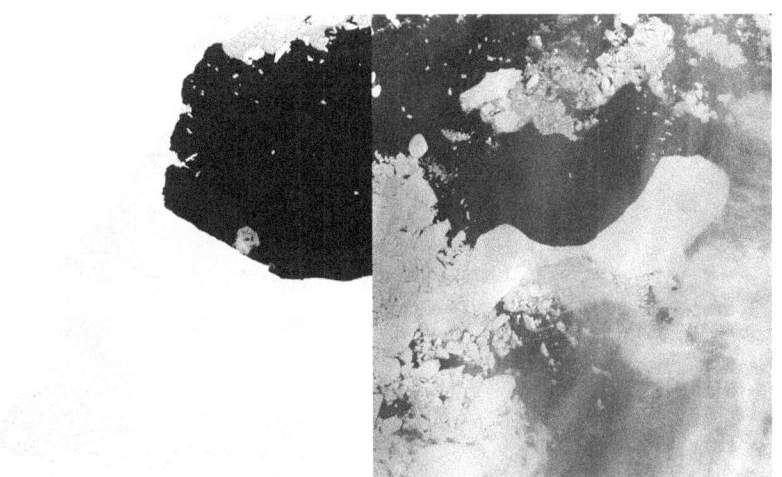

Activities

1. **Warm-up**: Visit the NASA webpage "Ice Shelf Collapse in East Antarctica" to view the before and after images of the ice shelf. As you toggle between the images, what do you notice?
2. **Before Reading the Poem**: View this map of Native American Land. What do you notice about the map as it changes?
3. **Reading the Poem**: Silently read "Map" by Linda Hogan. What do you notice about the poem? Note any words, phrases, or poetic structures that stand out to you and any questions you might have.
4. **Listening to the Poem**: Enlist two volunteers and listen as the poem is read aloud twice. What did you hear that you did not previously notice when you were reading the poem? Write down any additional words and phrases that stood out to you.
5. **Small Group Discussion**: Take turns sharing what you noticed in the poem with a small group. Based on the details you just shared and the discussions from the beginning of class, how does the map depicted in the poem compare to images you viewed earlier and to the map of Native American Land?
6. **Large Group Discussion**: How is this poem related to environmental justice? How does the map in the poem change over time? What happens to the ice in the second part of the poem?
7. **Extension for Grades 7–8**: What would a map of the poem look like? Draw it using lines from the poem.
8. **Extension for Grades 9–12**: Research what environmental justice or injustice looks like in your community, as well as the community leaders responsible for these issues. Write a letter to one or more of these leaders sharing what you have learned and your opinion about the issues.

More Context

Article

"Environmental justice (EJ) is the fair treatment and meaningful involvement of all people regardless of race, color, national origin, or income with respect to the development, implementation and enforcement of environmental laws, regulations and policies." Read the article "Learn About Environmental Justice" to understand how people can help protect the environment.

Glossary Term

Nature poetry poetry that engages with, describes, or considers the natural world.

"She Was Fed Turtle Soup"
by Lois Red Elk

The willows were turning green, slips of leafs pointing to one another in a slow tempo soothing the air with whispers of coming water. Her feet were bare and the earth cool while a loose hem feathered her ankles for her walk. Bracing on stems for the gradual pace to not disturb all the sleeping turtles, she wished for sunlight in a shade of green to hurry growth and to keep her hidden. How close could she lean into the memory of relatives who lived this life of damp shells and slow demeanor without alerting them of her intent. All of grandma's voices were now shaking her sleepy mind and begging her return to answer the details of her dream. It was the call of tradition that signaled the next step to seal the new experience into her life basket. She will be served turtle's energy for her growth. Off of grandma's favorite tree a knot was cut and shaped into a bowl. Handles in the shape of young turtles were carved into the sides. Into the cottonwood bowl was poured the prepared soup with essence of memory from a life once lived. Thanking all that came before this earth life, was her detailed prayer. A calling of all water animals to witness the taking of one energy to give to the energy of another, a child who passed the test of recalling ancient blood. Her heart will live with turtle strength. Her life will be long and purposefully directed. Her song will be like the cool breeze moving tall willows above eddies remembering motion.

Related Resource

About This Poem by Lois Red Elk

In the Dakota/Lakota culture, the story of the turtle carries a life of longevity and purposeful living. We make turtle amulets out of deerskin and present them to new mothers who have female babies. The prayer and promise with the amulet is that the child will have a long, purpose-filled life. A small portion of the baby's dried umbilical cord (the last connection between the mother and baby) is sewn into the amulet and kept with the child's clothing. The prayer and knowledge is that the turtle spirit now cares for the child spirit. Also, when the child matures and has their first dream, they are fed turtle soup. The dream is always good and reveals a lesson or purpose for the child. We celebrate with the child by telling them that the turtle spirit and energy, in the soup, is transferred into the child and will guide and protect the child in and through their dreams.

Illustration of a turtle.

Endicott, *[A turtle]*. Print, Library of Congress.

Activities

1. **Warm-up**: Use a computer or tablet to learn about the history of the Dakota/Lakota people. Taking turns, share what you learned with a partner.
2. **Before Reading the Poem**: Read the About This Poem statement written by Lois Red Elk and circle the words and phrases that stand out to you. In a small group, discuss why you think these traditions are important in the Dakota/Lakota culture. Cite evidence from the statement.
3. **Reading the Poem**: Silently read "She Was Fed Turtle Soup" by Lois Red Elk. What do you notice about the poem? Note any words, phrases, or poetic structures that stand out to you and any questions you might have.
4. **Listening to the Poem**: Enlist two volunteers and listen as the poem is read aloud twice. What did you hear that you did not previously notice when you were reading the poem? Write down any additional words and phrases that stood out to you.
5. **Small Group Discussion**: In a small group, take turns sharing a few of the words, phrases, and poetic structures that you noticed. Which words or phrases were mentioned most often? Why do you think these are important to the poem?
6. **Large Group Discussion**: Compare and contrast what you learned from the poet's statement and the poem. What did the poet tell us in one but not the other? What is your evidence?

7. **Extension for Grades 7–8**: Envision a coming of age tradition for your peers. What values would you include? What activities would you include? Why? Write about the tradition in either a poem or an essay.
8. **Extension for Grades 9–12**: Is there a coming of age tradition in your family's culture or history, or a coming of age tradition you've read or heard about? Research any rituals or activities associated with this tradition. What values are inherent in these rituals? Do you agree or disagree with these rituals and values? Why or why not? What might you change to make these rituals and values more agreeable to you? Write an essay about what this new tradition would look like, and defend your reasons for preserving or changing specific aspects.

More Context

Lecture

Read "Ancestors: A Mapping of Indigenous Poetry and Poets" in which Joy Harjo writes:

> The English language does not exist in a vacuum. Because it is an earthly creation of human communication, it is in a constant state of flux. English is renewed by use, especially by poets who have one of the most intimate relationships with it. The language then becomes a keeper, if you will, of cultural movement, ideas—a storehouse. For many indigenous poets, it is poetry that makes a bridge between indigenous spoken traditions and written English texts.

Glossary Term

Form the structure of a poem, including its line lengths, line breaks, meter, stanza lengths, and rhyme schemes.

"Instructions on Not Giving Up"
by Ada Limón

More than the fuchsia funnels breaking out
of the crabapple tree, more than the neighbor's
almost obscene display of cherry limbs shoving
their cotton candy-colored blossoms to the slate
sky of Spring rains, it's the greening of the trees
that really gets to me. When all the shock of white
and taffy, the world's baubles and trinkets, leave
the pavement strewn with the confetti of aftermath,
the leaves come. Patient, plodding, a green skin
growing over whatever winter did to us, a return
to the strange idea of continuous living despite
the mess of us, the hurt, the empty. Fine then,
I'll take it, the tree seems to say, a new slick leaf
unfurling like a fist to an open palm, I'll take it all.

Related Resource

Read the phoenix entry in the *Encyclopaedia Britannica*.

Illustration of two phoenixes.

Latin bestiary, *Phoenix plucking at vegetation (left) and lying in flames waiting to be reborn from the ashes (right)*, 12th century. Illustration, Encyclopædia Britannica.

Activities

1. **Warm-up**: Write down any associations you have with the concept of not giving up. Take turns sharing these with a partner.
2. **Before Reading the Poem**: Read the phoenix entry in the *Encyclopaedia Britannica* and write down the details you think are important. Talk to your partner about what you both have learned. What do you think might be the message of this myth?
3. **Reading the Poem**: Silently read "Instructions on Not Giving Up" by Ada Limón. What do you notice about the poem? Note any words, phrases, or poetic structures that stand out to you and any questions you might have.
4. **Listening to the Poem**: Enlist two volunteers and listen as the poem is read aloud twice. What did you hear that you did not previously notice when you were reading the poem? Write down any additional words and phrases that stood out to you.
5. **Small Group Discussion**: With a small group, take turns sharing what you noticed about the words, phrases, and poetic structures in the poem. Why do you think the speaker in the poem focuses on the greening of trees? What in the poem makes you think this is the case?
6. **Large Group Discussion**: What is the relationship between the poem and the phoenix myth? What images are used in the poem and the myth? How are the poem and the myth similar? How are they different?
7. **Extension for Grades 7–8**: Limón's poem is a sonnet. If you aren't familiar with the sonnet form, read about it in the glossary. Using the list of associations with the concept of not giving up from the earlier activity and other images you might think of, write a sonnet encouraging someone to keep their spirits up.
8. **Extension for Grades 9–12**: Write your own myth about not giving up. It can be based on a true story or something you have imagined. Use the list of associations you have from the beginning of this lesson to help you.

More Context

Article

The *Encyclopaedia Britannica* entry on the phoenix states, "Myth has existed in every society. Indeed, it would seem to be a basic constituent of human culture. Because the variety is so great, it is difficult to generalize about the nature of myths." Read the full definition and more about elements of mythology.

Glossary Term

Sonnet a fourteen-line poem, traditionally written in iambic pentameter, that employs one of several rhyme schemes and adheres to a tightly structured thematic organization.

"The Silver Thread"
by Afaa Michael Weaver

The fern gathers where the water seldom goes
unless the storms swell this world of wise choices,
the loud trickle of clear tongues of the stream
licking the edges of rock, while up ahead a curve
hides tomorrow from our crystal ball, the thing
we are afraid to admit we have, the guarantee
we hide from faith. In the woods our dog is lost
from time to time, until suddenly we hear her paws
inside winter's death becoming the yearly promise
of new undergrowth, her careless paws that beg
each day for the next bowl of treats, true faith
in what love yields. The rain stops not long after
it threatens to soak us with cold and chills, the trees
open to the gradual break of blue inside the gray,
turning the clouds naked and white under the sun,
the stream disappears under a bridge made by men
so trucks can crawl back and forth over this road
of dirt with its one row of grass, where our tongues
make a silver thread finding its way past the fear.

Related Resource

Clouds and landscape.

Thomas Cole, *Clouds*, ca. 1838. Oil on paper laid down on canvas, Metropolitan Museum of Art.

Activities

1. **Warm-up**: Write about how you feel on a rainy day in winter.
2. **Before Reading the Poem**: Look closely at the painting *Clouds*. Take plenty of time to look at the image carefully and write down the details you see, paying particular attention to colors, brush strokes, and the positioning of objects within the image. With a partner, take turns sharing what you noticed. How does the image make you feel? Do different parts of the image evoke different feelings? What do you think the painter did to evoke these feelings?
3. **Reading the Poem**: Silently read "The Silver Thread" by Afaa Michael Weaver. What do you notice about the poem? Note any words, phrases, or poetic structures that stand out to you and any questions you might have.
4. **Listening to the Poem**: Play the audio of Afaa Michael Weaver reading his poem twice or enlist two volunteers and listen as the poem is read aloud twice. What did you hear that you did not previously notice when you were reading the poem? Write down any additional words and phrases that stood out to you.
5. **Small Group Discussion**: In a small group, compile a list of the images you think are important in this poem. How do these images make you feel? How do your feelings change from the beginning of the poem to the end? What moments in the poem cause these changes in feeling? What did the poet do to make your feelings change?
6. **Large Group Discussion**: What do you think the story of this poem is? What images do you base this interpretation on? What is the "silver thread" the title references? What evidence do you have from your lists and discussions?
7. **Extension for Grades 7–8**: Come up with your own images for despair, faith, or love. Write a poem of 10 to 14 lines and use these images to create a story that gets better toward the end.
8. **Extension for Grades 9–12**: Carefully read "This Morning, This First Poem" by Afaa Michael Weaver. Note the images, phrases, and poetic structures that stand out to you. Write an essay in which you compare and contrast this poem with "The Silver Thread." Do you think one poem is more effective than the other? Why or why not? Provide evidence from the poems to support your response.

More Context
An Extended Biography of Afaa Michael Weaver

Afaa Michael Weaver was born Michael S. Weaver in Baltimore, Maryland, in 1951. The son of working class parents, he attended public schools and graduated high school as a National Merit finalist at the age of 16. After two years at the University of Maryland, he took a factory job alongside his father and uncles and remained a factory worker for 15 years. During this period, he wrote and published poetry, short fiction, and freelance journalism; he also founded 7th Son Press and the literary journal *Blind Alleys*.

Weaver's first book of poetry, *Water Song* (Callaloo Journal), was published in 1985. Six months after signing the contract, he received a fellowship from the National Endowment for the Arts and left the factory to attend Brown University's graduate writing program on a full university fellowship. He received an MA in theater and playwriting at Brown, while simultaneously completing a BA in literature at Excelsior College.

Since *Water Song*, Weaver has published several collections of poetry, including *Spirit Boxing* (University of Pittsburgh Press, 2017); *City of Eternal Spring* (University of Pittsburgh Press, 2014); *The Government of Nature* (University of Pittsburgh Press, 2013), for which he received the Kingsley Tufts Poetry Award; and *The Ten Lights of God* (Bucknell University Press, 2000). His full-length play *Rosa* was produced in 1993 at Venture Theater in Philadelphia. His short fiction has appeared in multiple anthologies, including *Children of the Night: The Best Short Stories by Black Writers, 1967 to the Present* (Little, Brown, 1997), edited by Gloria Naylor. In 2023, Weaver received the Academy of American Poets' Wallace Stevens Award.

Glossary Term

Anthropomorphism the attribution of human form, traits, actions, or emotions to an animal, object, or nonhuman being.

"Complaint of El Rio Grande"
by Richard Blanco

I was meant for all things to meet:
to make the clouds pause in the mirror
of my waters, to be home to fallen rain
that finds its way to me, to turn eons
of loveless rock into lovesick pebbles
and carry them as humble gifts back
to the sea which brings life back to me.

I felt the sun flare, praised each star
flocked about the moon long before
you did. I've breathed air you'll never
breathe, listened to songbirds before
you could speak their names, before
you dug your oars in me, before you
created the gods that created you.

Then countries—your invention—maps
jigsawing the world into colored shapes
caged in bold lines to say: you're here,
not there, you're this, not that, to say:
yellow isn't red, red isn't black, black is
not white, to say: mine, not ours, to say
war, and believe life's worth is relative.

You named me big river, drew me—blue,
thick to divide, to say: spic and Yankee,
to say: wetback and gringo. You split me
in two—half of me us, the rest them. But
I wasn't meant to drown children, hear
mothers' cries, never meant to be your
geography: a line, a border, a murderer.

I was meant for all things to meet:
the mirrored clouds and sun's tingle,
birdsongs and the quiet moon, the wind
and its dust, the rush of mountain rain—
and us. Blood that runs in you is water
flowing in me, both life, the truth we
know we know: be one in one another.

Related Resource

Child on the shore of the Rio Grande River.

Carol M. Highsmith, *Stroller on the shoreline of the Rio Grande River in Big Bend National Park, Texas*, 2014. Photograph, Library of Congress.

Activities

1. **Warm-up**: Imagine you are a river. Quickly write down the things you would see, taste, hear, and feel. Take turns sharing what you have written with a partner.
2. **Before Reading the Poem**: Look carefully at the photo of a child walking on the shoreline of the Rio Grande. Aside from the child, what do you notice? Make sure you look carefully at the entire photo. Write down what you see.
3. **Reading the Poem**: Silently read "Complaint of El Rio Grande" by Richard Blanco. What do you notice about the poem? Note any words, phrases, or poetic structures that stand out to you and any questions you might have.
4. **Listening to the Poem**: Enlist two volunteers and listen as the poem is read aloud twice. What did you hear that you did not previously notice when you were reading the poem? Write down any additional words and phrases that stood out to you.
5. **Small Group Discussion**: Call back the lines you like in the poem by saying these lines aloud with a partner and another pair of participants. Based on the lines you just shared with your small group, discuss how the first two stanzas in the poem relate to what you noticed in the photograph of the child at the river. Why might it be important to include these details in the poem?
6. **Large Group Discussion**: How does the poem change in the third and fourth stanzas? How are the earlier details in the poem woven together in the last stanza? What is the river telling us in the last stanza? Use what you've noticed in the poem to support your thoughts.

7. **Extension for Grades 7–8**: Write a poem imagining you are a river, and you are saying something important to the reader. Or pick something else—a cloud, a pebble, the sun, the moon, a songbird, the child, the mother, etc.—from the poem and give it a voice. Use your list of sensations from the warm-up to help you write this poem.
8. **Extension for Grades 9–12**: You might want to look at a map of the Rio Grande before you start this activity. Why is the Rio Grande an important river? What is the river referring to when it says, "I wasn't meant to drown children, hear / mother's cries, never meant to be your / geography: a line, a border, a murderer"? What does the river say it was meant for? What does it mean to "be one in one another"? Using specific examples from nature or urban life, write an essay that supports this idea.

More Context

Interview

Richard Blanco said:

> [Poetry] helps us understand our lives and the lives of others, who on the surface may seem very different from us. But, at its heart, poetry seeks the common human ground of the emotions we all share, it seeks dialogue, regardless of the particulars of any one ethnicity, race, sexuality, etc. Poetry makes us better humans, and a better human is a better doctor or lawyer, teacher or flight attendant, truck driver or cashier, parent, or sibling. A better anything. A better world, capable of ensuring our peace and survival.

Read more about his reflections about poetry in "An Interview with Education Ambassador Richard Blanco."

Glossary Term

Personification the attribution of human qualities to animals, inanimate objects, or abstract ideas.

Part 3: Past

"Coyote"
by Alexander Posey

A few days more, and then
There'll be no secret glen,
Or hollow, deep and dim,
To hide or shelter him.

And on the prairie far,
Beneath the beacon star
On evening's dark'ning shore,
I'll hear him nevermore.

For where the tepee smoke
Curled up of yore, the stroke
Of hammers rings all day,
And grim Doom shouts, "Make way!"

The immemorial hush
Is broken by the rush
Of armed enemies
Unto the utmost seas.

Related Resource

Read a brochure from Project Coyote.

Coexisting with coyotes brochure.

Project Coyote, "Coexisting with Coyotes," 2015. Screenshot from brochure, Project Coyote.

Activities

1. **Warm-up**: Think about any wild or urban animals you might occasionally see where you live or go to school. These can also be animals you know about from television, movies, or reading. Write about what you think their lives are like. How do you think their lives would have been different in the late 1800s?
2. **Before Reading the Poem**: Read the brochure from Project Coyote to learn about coyotes and how we coexist with them.
3. **Reading the Poem**: Silently read "Coyote" by Alexander Posey. What do you notice about the poem? Note any words, phrases, or poetic structures that stand out to you and any questions you might have.
4. **Listening to the Poem**: Enlist two volunteers and listen as the poem is read aloud twice. What did you hear that you did not previously notice when you were reading the poem? Write down any additional words and phrases that stood out to you.
5. **Small Group Discussion**: Take turns sharing what you noticed in the poem with a small group of participants. Based on the details you just shared, how does the poem relate to the brochure? What do you think the coyote represents to the speaker? Why?

6. **Large Group Discussion**: How does the tone of the poem change in the second half? What happens at the end of the poem? Who are the enemies? What is the rhyme scheme in this poem, and how does it affect your reading experience? How does rhyme play into oral tradition and memorization? If you aren't familiar with the ballad form, read the definition in the glossary.
7. **Extension for Grades 7–8**: Read the article "Removing Native Americans from their Land." What happens to the speaker and their community after "the rush / of armed enemies" descends? Write the next part of the poem.
8. **Extension for Grades 9–12**: In a 2015 lecture by former United States Poet Laureate Joy Harjo titled "Ancestors: A Mapping of Indigenous Poetry and Poets," Harjo states:

> It occurred to me that we have poetry ancestors. That thought was a door that made a fresh path of understanding. Each of us carries human ancestors within us. The DNA spiral is ancestral stories and songs. Even the stones, plants, elements, and creatures have ancestors. Each poem has ancestors, and maybe even an origin story.

With a partner or small group, create a visual map that connects Posey to other poets. Or create a visual map of your own poetry ancestors. Take turns sharing your visual maps with a group.

More Context

Essay

Read about native poetics in the essay "A Poetry Portfolio: Featuring Five of Our Country's Finest Native Poets," in which Natalie Diaz writes, "Native poetry is a crafted, honed, learned art, requiring skill. It is a choice made with great consideration—to use the white space that once silenced us as a platform to speak loudly."

Glossary Term

Quatrain a four-line stanza, or unit of four lines of verse, rhymed or unrhymed.

"Peace Path"
by Heid E. Erdrich

This path our people walked
one hundred two hundred   endless years
since the tall grass opened for us
and we breathed the incense that sun on prairie
                              offers to sky

Peace offering with each breath
each footstep   out of woods
to grasslands plotted with history
removal   remediation   restoration

Peace flag of fringed prairie orchid
green glow within white froth
calling a moth who nightly
seeks the now-rare scent   invisible to us

invisible history of this place
where our great-grandfather   a boy
beside two priests and 900 warriors
gaze intent in an 1870 photo
                            his garments white as orchids

Peace flag   white banner with red cross
crowned with thorns   held by a boy
at the elbow of a priest
beside Ojibwe warriors   beside Dakota warriors

Peace offered after smoke and dance
and Ojibwe gifts of elaborate beaded garments
thrown back in refusal   *torn with grief*
by Dakota Warriors   *since their brother's murder*

This is the path our people ran
through white flags of prairie plants
Ojibwe calling Dakota back
to sign one last and unbroken treaty

Peace offering with each breath
each footstep   out of woods
to grasslands plotted with history
removal   remediation   restoration

Two Dakota   *held up as great men*
humbled themselves
to an offer of peace
before a long walk south

before our people entered the trail
walking west and north
                            where you walk now

where we seek the source

the now-rare scent
invisible as history
history the tall grass opens for us
                        Breathe the incense of sun on prairie
                        Offer peace to the sky

Related Resource

Prairie path.

Unknown artist, *Untitled*, 2017. Photograph, Pxhere.

Activities

1. **Warm-up**: Make a list of different gestures and symbols that make you think about peace. Share your list with a partner.
2. **Before Reading the Poem**: Look at this photograph of a path. What specifically do you notice? What perspective is the photograph taken from? Can you imagine a place where the path might be leading? How might going down this path make you feel? Why? Taking turns, share your answers with a partner.
3. **Reading the Poem**: Silently read "Peace Path" by Heid E. Erdrich. What do you notice about the poem? Note any words, phrases, or poetic structures that stand out to you and any questions you might have.
4. **Listening to the Poem**: Enlist two volunteers and listen as the poem is read aloud twice. What did you hear that you did not previously notice when you were reading the poem? Write down any additional words and phrases that stood out to you.
5. **Small Group Discussion**: In a small group, take turns sharing what you noticed from reading and listening to the poem. How is the poem structured? Why do you think the poet structured it this way? Is any part of the poem repeated, perhaps with slight changes? Why do you think the poet repeated these words?

6. **Large Group Discussion**: How does the structure of the poem relate to its content and the photograph of the path? What history might be recounted in this poem? What in the poem tells you this? How does the imagery of the tall grass make you feel at the beginning of the poem, and do you feel differently when the same imagery is repeated at the end?
7. **Extension for Grades 7–8**: Research the Ojibwe and Dakota tribes and their histories. Write an essay about what you have learned.
8. **Extension for Grades 9–12**: Is it possible to look at the left and right sides of the poem as separate poems or as halves of the same story? How might they be seen as two separate poems? What are the similarities and differences between the stories they tell? If you look at the two sides as part of one poem, how do they interact with each other in content and structure? Give an oral presentation about your thoughts to a small group.

More Context

About this Poem

by Heid E. Erdrich

The North Country Trail leaves Minnesota and heads toward Fort Abercrombie just above my hometown—Wahpeton, North Dakota. This poem envisions the tallgrass prairie as I have seen last remaining swaths of it in areas of the trail. The poem depicts events that took place when the grassland was unbroken and when our great-grandfather, Keesh-ke-mun-ishiw/Joseph Gourneau, serving as an altar boy and standard bearer for a Catholic priest, was photographed at Fort Abercrombie in 1870.

The path the North Country Trail traces from the Lake Superior shore through the North Dakota grasslands, maps the migration of my Ojibwe ancestors as they moved, and were removed, from their territories as treaties decreed. For me, and for other Native Americans, a map of the trail tells a specific story, one of tribal history.

The Grasslands stand as an emblem of peace for me—the hush of wind in tall grasses, the surprise of wild roses and rare lilies, the open faces of sunflowers in fields, the prairie potholes where water is life and the home of thousands of birds—this peace, like the weathered wooden structures of previous centuries, remains for everyone to walk by along the western section of the North Country Trail.

Glossary Term

Contrapuntal a poetic form that interweaves two or more poems to create a single poem that can be read in multiple ways depending on how the poem is designed on the page.

"Binsey Poplars"
by Gerard Manley Hopkins

felled 1879

My aspens dear, whose airy cages quelled,
  Quelled or quenched in leaves the leaping sun,
  All felled, felled, are all felled;
    Of a fresh and following folded rank
      Not spared, not one
      That dandled a sandalled
    Shadow that swam or sank
On meadow and river and wind-wandering weed-winding bank.
  O if we but knew what we do
    When we delve or hew—
  Hack and rack the growing green!
    Since country is so tender
  To touch, her being só slender,
  That, like this sleek and seeing ball
  But a prick will make no eye at all,
  Where we, even where we mean
    To mend her we end her,
    When we hew or delve:
After-comers cannot guess the beauty been.
  Ten or twelve, only ten or twelve
    Strokes of havoc únselve
      The sweet especial scene,
    Rural scene, a rural scene,
    Sweet especial rural scene.

Related Resource

Allée of poplar trees.

Vincent van Gogh, *Poplars near Nuenen*, 1885. Painting, Museum Boijmans Van Beuningen.

Activities

1. **Warm-up:** Look carefully at the image of the painting *Poplars Near Nuenen* by Vincent van Gogh. Write down the details you notice in the painting.
2. **Before Reading the Poem:** Talk to a partner about what you noticed. How does Van Gogh represent light in the poplars, and what overall role do the poplars play in the landscape? Use the details you noticed to back up your answers.
3. **Reading the Poem:** Silently read "Binsey Poplars" by Gerard Manley Hopkins. What do you notice about the poem? Note any words, phrases, or poetic structures that stand out to you and any questions you might have.
4. **Listening to the Poem:** Enlist two volunteers and listen as the poem is read aloud twice. What did you hear that you did not previously notice when you were reading the poem? Write down any additional words and phrases that stood out to you.
5. **Small Group Discussion:** In a small group, take turns sharing the details you noticed in the painting and the poem. Develop a list of important details together.
6. **Large Group Discussion:** Based on your small group discussions, how does Hopkins use the sound of words to help us understand how he feels about the poplars? How does Van Gogh use brush strokes to demonstrate how he feels about poplars? Make sure you indicate specific brush strokes and colors.
7. **Extension for Grades 7–8:** As you continue to think about the poem and the painting, how might Hopkins and Van Gogh feel about today's environmental movement? Write a script in which you imagine a dialogue between them that discusses how they feel. Use details from the poem and painting.
8. **Extension for Grades 9–12:** Gerard Manley Hopkins often used alliterative and rhyming language in his poetry. Write a poem that shows how you feel about the natural environment using alliteration, rhyme, and strong imagery. It's important to show the reader how you feel, rather than tell the reader how you feel.

More Context

Nature Poems

Read a selection of poems about nature, wildlife, and the outdoors such as "Pursuit" by Elizabeth Bradfield, "Patience Taught by Nature" by Elizabeth Barrett Browning, and more.

Glossary Term

Alliteration the repetition of consonant sounds, particularly at the beginning of words.

"The Snowfall Is So Silent"
by Miguel de Unamuno and translated by Ricardo Alberto Maldonado

The snowfall is silent,
a slow thing;
little by little, with softness,
it settles over the land
and covers the fields.
White and weightless,
the silent snow settles;
the snowfall makes no noise;
it falls as if forgetting,
flake by flake.
It softens then fields it blankets
while the ice harasses them,
with flashes of white;
blanketing everything with a pure,
silent covering;
no small thing on the ground
escapes it.
Wherever it falls it stays,
weightless and content,
for snow does not slide off
like rain does,
but stays and seeps in.
Flakes are sky flowers,
white lilies from clouds,
wearing themselves out on ground,
they come down flowering,
but so suddenly
they melt;
blooming only on the peaks,
above mountains,
weariness over the earth,
and dying on the inside.
Snow, soft snow,
that falls with such lightness
on the head,
over the heart,
come and cover my sadness,
which lays rest in my reason.

La nevada es silenciosa

La nevada es silenciosa,
cosa lenta;
poco a poco y con blandura
reposa sobre la tierra
y cobija a la llanura.
Posa la nieve callada
blanca y leve;
la nevada no hace ruido;
cae como cae el olvido,
copo a copo.
Abriga blanda a los campos
cuando el hielo los hostiga;
con sus lampos de blancura;
cubre a todo con su capa
pura, silenciosa;
no se le escapa en el suelo
cosa alguna.
Donde cae allí se queda
leda y leve,
pues la nieve no resbala
como resbala la lluvia,
sino queda y cala.
Flores del cielo los copos,
blancos lirios de las nubes,
que en el suelo se ajan,
bajan floridos,
pero quedan pronto
derretidos;
florecen sólo en la cumbre,
sobre las montañas,
pesadumbre de la tierra,
y en sus entrañas perecen.
Nieve, blanda nieve,
la que cae tan leve
sobre la cabeza,
sobre el corazón,
ven y abriga mi tristeza
la que descansa en razón.

Part 3

Related Resource

Snow on mountains.

John Singer Sargent, *Snow*, ca. 1909–11. Watercolor and graphite, Metropolitan Museum of Art.

Activities

1. **Warm-up**: Look carefully at John Singer Sargent's watercolor *Snow*. What do you notice about how Sargent painted the snow? What do the brush strokes and lines look like? Make a list of what you see.
2. **Before Reading the Poem**: Take turns with a partner discussing how this painting makes you feel about snow. Talk about the techniques you think Sargent used to make you feel this way.
3. **Reading the Poem**: Silently read "The Snowfall Is So Silent" by Miguel de Unamuno, translated by Ricardo Alberto Maldonado. If you understand both Spanish and English, read the poem in both languages. What do you notice about the poem? Note any words, phrases, or poetic structures that stand out to you and any questions you might have.
4. **Listening to the Poem**: Enlist two volunteers and listen as the poem is read aloud twice. What did you hear that you did not previously notice when you were reading the poem? Write down any additional words and phrases that stood out to you. If you know Spanish, read the poem aloud in both languages. What did you notice when the poem was read aloud this way?
5. **Small Group Discussion**: In a small group, take turns sharing the words, phrases, and poetic structures you noted from the poem. How does the poem make you feel about snow? How do you think the speaker is feeling? What is he thinking? Cite evidence from the

words, phrases, and poetic structures you just discussed to support what you think and how you feel.
6. **Large Group Discussion**: Based on the image, the poem, and your discussion about what you saw and felt, what are several ways people can think and feel about snow? How are the painting and the poem similar and different?
7. **Extension for Grades 7–8**: Draw or paint a picture of a snowy scene. Make sure the picture shows how you feel. Then write a haiku that portrays the scene you have created. Add the haiku to the sheet of paper with your scene and give them both a title. Take turns sharing your scene and haiku with a small group. You can find the definition of a haiku in the glossary.
8. **Extension for Grades 9–12**: Browse this collection of essays on translation found on Poets.org. Read several essays and present what you've learned about translation to a small group of people.

More Context

Article

Claire Cleveland and Andrea Dukakis write in "Yes, It Really Is Quieter When It Snows. Here's the Science behind the Calm after the Storm":

> Not just any snow can trap noise. It has to be the freshly fallen, light and fluffy. Wet and heavy snow doesn't leave those spaces for sound to be trapped. One study found a couple of inches of snow can absorb as much as 60 percent of sound. Snow can act as a commercial sound-absorbing foam when it's in that fluffy, freshly fallen state.

Read more of the article and the research study that it references.

Glossary Term

Translation the art of transferring meaning from one language to another.

"To Winter"
by Claude McKay

Stay, season of calm love and soulful snows!
There is a subtle sweetness in the sun,
The ripples on the stream's breast gaily run,
The wind more boisterously by me blows,
And each succeeding day now longer grows.
The birds a gladder music have begun,
The squirrel, full of mischief and of fun,
From maples' topmost branch the brown twig throws.
I read these pregnant signs, know what they mean:
I know that thou art making ready to go.
Oh stay! I fled a land where fields are green
Always, and palms wave gently to and fro,
And winds are balmy, blue brooks ever sheen,
To ease my heart of its impassioned woe.

Related Resource

Snowy cityscape.

Detroit Publishing Co., *What sorcery within a night has made a city street into a fairy glade?*, 1900–10. Dry plate negatives, Library of Congress.

Activities

1. **Warm-up**: How do you feel about winter? Why? Share your thoughts with a partner.
2. **Before Reading the Poem**: Look carefully at the photograph of a snowy city street. What do you notice in the image? Look again. What else do you see? How does it make you feel?

3. **Reading the Poem**: Silently read "To Winter" by Claude McKay. What do you notice about the poem? Note any words, phrases, or poetic structures that stand out to you and any questions you might have.
4. **Listening to the Poem**: Enlist two volunteers and listen as the poem is read aloud twice. What did you hear that you did not previously notice when you were reading the poem? Write down any additional words and phrases that stood out to you.
5. **Small Group Discussion**: With a small group, take turns sharing the words, phrases, and poetic structures that stood out to you in the poem. How do you think the speaker feels about winter? How do you feel about winter?
6. **Large Group Discussion**: Is this poem an ode? Why or why not? How does the tone of the poem change at the end of the poem? How would you describe the speaker?
7. **Extension for Grades 7–8**: Based on the activities and what you have learned, create a poem and illustration that show how you feel about winter. What do you want to communicate before the new year or spring? How can you depict that in your poem?
8. **Extension for Grades 9–12**: Choose another poem about winter to read and recite. Think about how you can express emotion during your reading. Memorize and recite the poem for your group. After, discuss what it was like to memorize and recite a poem.

More Context

Article

> When considering essential movements in American poetry, no conversation would be complete without a discussion of the Harlem Renaissance. With a lyricism seated in the popular blues and jazz music of the time, an awareness of Black life in America, its assertion of an independent African American identity, and its innovation in form and structure, the poetry of the Harlem Renaissance is unmistakable.

Read more about this essential poetic movement in "A Brief Guide to the Harlem Renaissance."

Glossary Term

Volta a rhetorical shift that marks the change of a thought or argument in a poem.

"Maggie and Milly and Molly and May"
by E. E. Cummings

maggie and milly and molly and may
went down to the beach(to play one day)

and maggie discovered a shell that sang
so sweetly she couldn't remember her troubles, and

milly befriended a stranded star
whose rays five languid fingers were;

and molly was chased by a horrible thing
which raced sideways while blowing bubbles:and

may came home with a smooth round stone
as small as a world and as large as alone.

For whatever we lose(like a you or a me)
it's always ourselves we find in the sea

Related Resource

Ocean Beach, San Francisco.

Esther Cuan, *Ocean and waves*, 2016. Photograph, Unsplash.

Activities
1. **Warm-up**: Look carefully at the photograph of the beach. Imagine you are standing or sitting in front of the waves. What would you see? Hear? Smell? Write down what you imagine.
2. **Before Reading the Poem**: With a partner, take turns sharing what you wrote. Write down any associations with sitting at the beach that you have in common.

3. **Reading the Poem**: Silently read "maggie and milly and molly and may" by E. E. Cummings. What do you notice about the poem? Note any words, phrases, or poetic structures that stand out to you and any questions you might have.
4. **Listening to the Poem**: Enlist two volunteers and listen as the poem is read aloud twice. What did you hear that you did not previously notice when you were reading the poem? Write down any additional words and phrases that stood out to you.
5. **Small Group Discussion**: In a small group, share what you noticed when you read and listened to the poem. What happened to each of the people in the poem when they went to the beach? Do you think they expected what happened to happen?
6. **Large Group Discussion**: Do you agree with the last two lines of the poem? Use details you noticed in the poem to support your position.
7. **Extension for Grades 7–8**: Write a poem about a visit you took to the beach or to another place that you love in the natural world. Write five to ten couplets using words that describe what you see, hear, and smell. Make sure that what you write shows the reader how you feel about this place.
8. **Extension for Grades 9–12**: E. E. Cummings uses rhyme, slant rhyme, alliteration, and couplets in this poem. If you aren't familiar with these terms, you can find them in the glossary. Using at least two of these poetic techniques, write a poem based on the line "it's always ourselves we find in the sea."

More Context

Resource

From whales to starfish and corals and seabirds, learn more about marine wildlife by reading the "Marine Life Encyclopedia."

Glossary Term

Rhyme the correspondence of sounds in words or lines of verse.

"Willow Poem"
by William Carlos Williams

It is a willow when summer is over,
a willow by the river
from which no leaf has fallen nor
bitten by the sun
turned orange or crimson.
The leaves cling and grow paler,
swing and grow paler
over the swirling waters of the river
as if loath to let go,
they are so cool, so drunk with
the swirl of the wind and of the river—
oblivious to winter,
the last to let go and fall
into the water and on the ground.

Related Resource

Listen to musical legend Billie Holiday sing the song "Willow Weep for Me," written by Ann Ronell.

Billie Holiday.

Unnamed, *Los Angeles Times* photographer, 1949. Photograph, UCLA Library.

Activities

1. **Warm-up**: Listen to the recording of Billie Holiday singing "Willow Weep for Me" twice. The first time, just listen. After, write down what you remember about the willow and the image of it you have in your head. Note how you feel. While listening to the song a second time, note the images that stand out to you.
2. **Before Reading the Poem**: Based on your experience listening to the song, with a partner take turns creating a tableau (a picture using your body) that depicts the willow tree. Make sure to note what you see when your partner creates their tree tableau.
3. **Reading the Poem**: Silently read "Willow Poem" by William Carlos Williams. What do you notice about the poem? Note any words, phrases, or poetic structures that stand out to you and any questions you might have.
4. **Listening to the Poem**: Enlist two volunteers and listen as the poem is read aloud twice. What did you hear that you did not previously notice when you were reading the poem? Write down any additional words and phrases that stood out to you.
5. **Small Group Discussion**: Based on what you have read, heard, and seen, what image of a willow tree is William Carlos Williams trying to create? In a small group, discuss how the willow in the poem and the willow tableaux you created with a partner make you feel.
6. **Large Group Discussion**: Use the notes you've taken to discuss the following questions: What did the willow in the song convey, and how did the song create this image? What did the willow in Williams's poem convey, and what words or phrases helped create this image?
7. **Extension for Grades 7–8**: Write a poem personifying a willow tree and talk about its life. Make sure to use images and feelings generated by your earlier activities.

8. **Extension Grades 9–12**: Read "A Brief Guide to Imagism." Create an oral presentation with your partner in which one of you argues for the importance of the imagist movement in poetry and the other argues against it. Make sure to use examples from imagist poems in your presentations.

More Context
Poetic Device

Personification describes when "human characteristics are attributed to an abstract quality, animal, or inanimate object." Read more of the definition and find examples of personification in the *Encyclopædia Britannica*.

Glossary Term

Imagery language in a poem that represents a sensory experience.

"Saint Francis and the Sow"
by Galway Kinnell

The bud
stands for all things,
even for those things that don't flower,
for everything flowers, from within, of self-blessing;
though sometimes it is necessary
to reteach a thing its loveliness,
to put a hand on its brow
of the flower
and retell it in words and in touch
it is lovely
until it flowers again from within, of self-blessing;
as Saint Francis
put his hand on the creased forehead
of the sow, and told her in words and in touch
blessings of earth on the sow, and the sow
began remembering all down her thick length,
from the earthen snout all the way
through the fodder and slops to the spiritual curl of the tail,
from the hard spininess spiked out from the spine
down through the great broken heart
to the sheer blue milken dreaminess spurting and shuddering
from the fourteen teats into the fourteen mouths sucking and
    blowing beneath them:
the long, perfect loveliness of sow.

Related Resource

Sow and five piglets.

Keith Weller, *Sow and five piglets*, 2006. Photograph, Agricultural Research Service.

Activities

1. **Warm-up**: Who was Saint Francis? If you don't know, conduct research about him.
2. **Before Reading the Poem**: Look carefully at the photograph "Sow and Five Piglets." Note that a sow in this context is an adult female pig. Write down what you see and your reaction to it. Take turns sharing your notes with a partner.
3. **Reading the Poem**: Silently read "Saint Francis and the Sow" by Galway Kinnell. What do you notice about the poem? Note any words, phrases, or poetic structures that stand out to you and any questions you might have.
4. **Listening to the Poem**: Enlist two volunteers and listen as the poem is read aloud twice. What did you hear that you did not previously notice when you were reading the poem? Write down any additional words and phrases that stood out to you.
5. **Small Group Discussion**: With your partner and another pair, take turns sharing the words, phrases, and poetic structures that stand out to you in the poem. What does Saint Francis do?
6. **Large Group Discussion**: How does the speaker in the poem feel about the sow at the end? What does the poet do to help us reach that conclusion? What point do you think the speaker is trying to make? Make sure you use what you noticed in the poem as evidence.
7. **Extension for Grades 7–8**: Do you think this poem is relevant for students today? If so, in what way? Have a debate with a partner in which one of you argues it has relevance and the other argues that it does not. Make sure to give evidence for your positions.
8. **Extension for Grades 9–12**: Research the poet Galway Kinnell. Read as many of his poems that interest you, and select one or two that you find particularly meaningful. Read these poems aloud in your small group and explain why they are meaningful to you, giving specific examples from the poem and from your experience.

More Context

Article

"In relation to a person's emotional rapport with an animal, is empathy possible?" asked M. W. Fox of the Humane Society of the United States in 1984. Read more of "Empathy, Humaneness and Animal Welfare" to discover how this question continues to remain important in understanding empathy and the relationship between people and animals.

Glossary Term

Allusion a reference to a person, event, or literary work.

"The Metier of Blossoming"
by Denise Levertov

Fully occupied with growing—that's
the amaryllis. Growing especially
at night: it would take
only a bit more patience than I've got
to sit keeping watch with it till daylight;
the naked eye could register every hour's
increase in height. Like a child against a barn door,
proudly topping each year's achievement,
steadily up
goes each green stem, smooth, matte,
traces of reddish purple at the base, and almost
imperceptible vertical ridges
running the length of them:
Two robust stems from each bulb,
sometimes with sturdy leaves for company,
elegant sweeps of blade with rounded points.
Aloft, the gravid buds, shiny with fullness.

One morning—and so soon!—the first flower
has opened when you wake. Or you catch it poised
in a single, brief
moment of hesitation.
Next day, another,
shy at first like a foal,
even a third, a fourth,
carried triumphantly at the summit
of those strong columns, and each
a Juno, calm in brilliance,
a maiden giantess in modest splendor.
If humans could be
that intensely whole, undistracted, unhurried,
swift from sheer
unswerving impetus! If we could blossom
out of ourselves, giving
nothing imperfect, withholding nothing!

Related Resource

Watch the video "Amaryllis Growing, Flowering and Decaying, Time-Lapse."

Time-lapse video of an amaryllis flower.

YouTube contributor, "Amaryllis Growing, Flowering and Decaying, Time-Lapse," posted Feb 9, 2010. Screenshot from video, YouTube.

Activities

1. **Warm-up**: Watch the video "Amaryllis Growing, Flowering and Decaying, Time-Lapse." Write down as many details as you can about the growth of the amaryllis. With a partner, take turns sharing your details.
2. **Before Reading the Poem**: Scan the poem "The Metier of Blossoming" by Denise Levertov for any words you do not know. Make sure to find out the meaning of these words before you read the poem.
3. **Reading the Poem**: Silently read "The Metier of Blossoming" by Denise Levertov. What do you notice about the poem? Note any words, phrases, or poetic structures that stand out to you and any questions you might have.
4. **Listening to the Poem**: Enlist two volunteers and listen as the poem is read aloud twice. What did you hear that you did not previously notice when you were reading the poem? Write down any additional words and phrases that stood out to you.
5. **Small Group Discussion**: What vivid words does Levertov use to describe the growth of the amaryllis? Take turns sharing these words in a small group. Try to agree on a list of the words that make you see the flower in your imagination.
6. **Large Group Discussion**: Why might the speaker in the poem say growth is the flower's métier? In what ways does Levertov compare and contrast human growth to amaryllis growth? What is your evidence from the poem?

7. **Extension for Grades 7–8**: Watch a segment of this video featuring curlews flying and singing. Using vivid words, describe the bird and its actions. Draw a picture of the bird that you can add to your written description.
8. **Extension for Grades 9–12**: What do you think is the métier of a bird? Watch a bird outside for 15 minutes. If you don't see a bird outside, watch another segment of the curlews video. Write down what you see. Describe the bird and its actions. Write a poem using vivid language that describes the bird, its métier, and how it is similar to or different from humans.

More Context

Extended Biography of Denise Levertov

After her move to the U.S. [in 1948], [Denise] Levertov was introduced to the Transcendentalism of Ralph Waldo Emerson and Henry David Thoreau, the formal experimentation of Ezra Pound, and, in particular, the work of William Carlos Williams. Through her husband's friendship with poet Robert Creeley, she became associated with the Black Mountain group of poets, particularly Creeley, Charles Olson, and Robert Duncan, who had formed a short-lived but groundbreaking school in 1933 in North Carolina. Some of Levertov's work was published in the 1950s in the *Black Mountain Review*. Levertov acknowledged these influences but disclaimed membership in any poetic school. She moved away from the fixed forms of English practice, developing an open, experimental style. Read more about Denise Levertov.

Glossary Term

Caesura a pause for a beat in the rhythm of a verse, often indicated by a line break or punctuation.

"Blessing the Boats"
by Lucille Clifton

(at St. Mary's)

may the tide
that is entering even now
the lip of our understanding
carry you out
beyond the face of fear
may you kiss
the wind then turn from it
certain that it will
love your back may you
open your eyes to water
water waving forever
and may you in your innocence
sail through this to that

Related Resource

Boats on a river.

Salomon van Ruysdael, *Marine*, 1650. Oil on wood, Metropolitan Museum of Art.

Activities

1. **Warm-up**: Look closely at the painting *Marine*. Write down the details you notice including colors, brushstrokes, etc. What do you think these details mean? How do they make you feel? Using what you've noticed, imagine what could happen to any of the boats sailing on the river.

2. **Before Reading the Poem**: With a partner, take turns sharing your notes about the painting and what you imagined could happen. Work together to arrive at a shared vision for the future of the sailboats as they travel on the river. Based on your notes and what you imagined, write down what you would say to the people on board the boats before they depart.
3. **Reading the Poem**: Silently read "blessing the boats" by Lucille Clifton. What do you notice about the poem? Note any words, phrases, or poetic structures that stand out to you and any questions you might have.
4. **Listening to the Poem**: Enlist two volunteers and listen as the poem is read aloud twice. What did you hear that you did not previously notice when you were reading the poem? Write down any additional words and phrases that stood out to you.
5. **Small Group Discussion**: What are the similarities and/or differences between what you would say to the people in the boats and what the speaker in the poem says?
6. **Large Group Discussion**: While the poem's audience might be people in boats, it can also be read as a metaphor for someone or something else. Using what you've noticed in the poem and painting as evidence, who or what might the sailors represent?
7. **Extension for Grades 7–8**: Create a storyboard based on who you think the sailors in the poem might represent. Include what you imagine would happen to them. Take turns sharing this with others.
8. **Extension for Grades 9–12**: The issue of climate change is one of the most important challenges facing our planet. What might you do to help make climate change a less serious threat? How might you sail "from this to that"? What is the speaker in "blessing the boats" telling you? Gather a group of people and present your thoughts to them.

More Context

Article

Learn about the basic physics principles of sailing, along with additional information for teaching the mechanics of sailing in the article, "An Introduction to the Physics of Sailing."

Glossary Term

Ode a lyric address to an event, a person, or a thing not present.

3 Glossary of Poetic Terms

Alliteration the repetition of consonant sounds, particularly at the beginning of words.

Alliteration describes multiple words grouped together that contain the same first consonant sound. Alliteration is used in common speech and all forms of literature, but it is especially prominent in poetry, which places emphasis on sound and the sound of words. A well-known example of alliteration is William Shakespeare's "Sonnet 30: When to the sessions of sweet silent thought." The words "sessions," "sweet," "silent," "summon," "sigh," and "sought" all begin with the same consonant sound and occur close together in the first three lines of the poem.

Allusion a reference to a person, event, or literary work.

Allusions are implied or indirect, and poems with allusions do not necessarily cite the work or historical event they are referencing. When poets use allusions, they are assuming a shared knowledge between themselves and the reader. Traditional Western literature often makes allusions to other works in literature, the Bible, and Greek mythology with the understanding that most readers will have experience with the texts. However, some poets intentionally use obscure allusions in their writing, knowing that few readers will understand the references. Allusions can be used to enhance a text by introducing context or background information.

Anaphora a poetic technique in which successive phrases or lines begin with the same words, often resembling a litany.

The term anaphora comes from the Greek for "a carrying up or back." As one of the oldest-known literary devices, anaphora is used in much of the world's religious and devotional poetry, including numerous biblical hymns in the *Book of Psalms*. The repetition of anaphora can be as simple as a single word or as long as an entire phrase. Anaphora can create a driving rhythm by the recurrence of the same sound, and it can also intensify the emotion of the poem.

Anthropomorphism the attribution of human form, traits, actions, or emotions to an animal, object, or nonhuman being.

The term anthropomorphism derives from the Greek word *anthrōpomorphos* meaning "having human form or qualities." Distinct from personification, anthropomorphism does not rely on figurative language to provide human attributes in a metaphorical or representative way. Instead, anthropomorphism is used to display human traits and attributes of human behavior in animals, objects, nonhuman, or supernatural beings incapable of having such characteristics. For example, Homer uses anthropomorphism in his epic poems *The Odyssey* and *The Iliad* by assigning human qualities and tendencies to Greek gods, including Aphrodite and Ares.

Ars poetica a poem that explores the art of poetry by examining the role of the poet and their relationship to the poem and the act of writing.

Among the first known treatises on poetry, Horace's "Ars Poetica," also referred to as "Epistle to the Pisos," is literally translated as "The Art of Poetry" or "On the Art of Poetry." Composed sometime between 20 BC and 13 BC, the poem outlines principles of poetry, including knowledge, decorum, and sincerity, and introduced Horace as both a poet and critic. While the focus of ars poetica has shifted from didactic argument toward more introspective takes on a poet's individual art, Horace's treatise continues to serve as the model for poets to examine their writing process and relationship to poetry.

Ballad a plot-driven song with one or more characters, often constructed in quatrain stanzas.

A ballad tends to show rather than tell the reader what's happening, describing each crucial moment in the trail of events as the poem leads to a dramatic conclusion. To convey a sense of emotional urgency, a ballad is often constructed in quatrain stanzas, each line containing as few as three or four stresses and either the second and fourth lines or all alternating lines rhyming. During the Renaissance, creating and selling ballad broadsides became a popular practice, and ballads began to make their way into print in 15th-century England from European folk tradition. The ballad has been used by acclaimed poets of various poetic movements from Romantic poet Emily Dickinson to Modernist poet Ezra Pound and beyond.

Caesura a pause for a beat in the rhythm of a verse, often indicated by a line break or by punctuation.

The term caesura comes from the Latin past participle stem of *caedere*, meaning "to cut down." There are three types of caesura: initial, medial, and terminal. Initial caesura is when the pause appears at or near the beginning of a line, medial caesura occurs in the middle of the line, and terminal caesura is when the pause appears at the end or near the end of a line. Historically, medial caesura was primarily used in many classical meters. Today, modern poetic forms and contemporary poets are flexible with the use of caesura.

See also meter.

Concrete poetry poetry that creates physical shapes with language; a concrete poem is as much a piece of visual art made with words as it is a work of poetry.

European artists Max Bill and Öyving Fahlström originated the term concrete poetry in the early 1950s. During this period, concrete poems were intended to be abstract and without allusion to a recognizable shape, like the E. E. Cummings' poem "r-p-o-p-h-e-s-s-a-g-r," which uses spacing and punctuation to create a distinct form on the page, but doesn't evoke any associations to an identifiable object. The movement spread, reached its height of popularity in the 1960s, and then the shape of the poems became less abstract. Poets began to adopt concrete poetry as a specific poetic form that used words, often the repetition of the same word, to depict a recognizable object, shape, or pattern. Contemporary concrete poetry has evolved to include photography, film, and even soundscapes.

Contrapuntal a poetic form that interweaves two or more poems to create a single poem that can be read in multiple ways depending on how the poem is designed on the page.

Contrapuntal comes from the Italian word *contrapunto*, which means "pertaining to counterpoint" and "backstitch." The poetic form is inspired by contrapuntal, or counterpoint, music, which is defined as the use of multiple independent melodies playing simultaneously with an equal weight on each so no melody dominates. Russian novelist and symbolist poet Andrei Bely is noted for employing the contrapuntal form and devices of music in his long poem "Pervoe Svidanie." Contrapuntal as a poetic form re-emerged in the 21st century in the work of poets such as Brian Bilston, Sarah Cooper, Tarfia Faizullah, and Tyehimba Jess. The theme of a contrapuntal poem varies, and there are no structural constraints of meter or rhyme. The key feature of contrapuntal poetry is how the poem appears on the page, thus sharing similar visual characteristics with concrete or shape poetry, as well as postmodern aesthetics.

Couplet a two-line stanza, or two successive lines of verse, rhymed or unrhymed.

In French, *couplet* is the diminutive of couple. In poetry, the two lines in a couplet can rhyme with one another and have the same meter, or not. Not all couplets have similar syllabic patterns. A couplet can be either open or closed. If open, a couplet is a run-on couplet, meaning the first line flows to the second as a continuous sentence. If closed, the couplet is a formal couplet featuring two separate sentences. A couplet can be part of a poem or be a poem on its own. A well-known type of couplet in English poetry is the heroic couplet, which is written in rhymed iambic pentameter.

See also line, meter, and stanza.

End-stopped line a metrical line that contains a complete phrase or sentence, or a poetic line that ends with punctuation.

End-stopped lines are the opposite of enjambed lines in that end-stopped lines contain complete thoughts, phrases, or sentences. These lines give the reader moments to pause at a line break. Usually, a poetic line is end-stopped if there is punctuation at the end. The punctuation could be internal (e.g., comma, semicolon, colon, em-dash) or external (e.g., period, exclamation mark, question mark). Many poets interweave end-stopped and enjambed lines in their poetry, whereas others will compose poems entirely of end-stopped lines.

Enjambment the continuation of a sentence or clause across a poetic line break.

Enjambment comes from the French word *enjamber*, which means "to stride over." Enjambment was first formally used in the mid-19th century, but the poetic device can be traced back to Biblical verses and the works of Homer. An enjambed line is the opposite of an end-stopped line, in that the running-over of a sentence or phrase across one poetic line to the next is done without punctuation, whereas an end-stopped line ends a poetic line with punctuation. Enjambed lines minimize the difference of sound between verse and prose and increase the speed and pacing of a poem. By the 20th century, enjambment became a key feature in poetry.

Epistolary poem a poem of direct address that reads as a letter; also known as an epistle.

Epistle derives from the Latin word *epistula* meaning letter. Epistolary poems are poems that read as letters. As poems of direct address, they can be intimate and colloquial or formal and measured. The subject matter can range from philosophical investigation to a declaration of love or a list of errands. Epistles can take any form, from heroic couplets to free verse.

Form the structure of a poem, including its line lengths, line breaks, meter, stanza lengths, and rhyme schemes.

Every poem has a form, but some forms are unique to individual poems and some are more widely used and include their own set of rules and parameters. Specific poetic forms include sonnet, villanelle, haiku, and prose poem. Form refers to the appearance and sound of the poem, but it can also influence the tone or purpose of the poem. For example, many sonnets are love poems, so the tone of a poem written in the sonnet form might be reverent or yearning. Although some forms observe specific rules, poets often break these rules to subvert readers' expectations so the deviation from a particular form becomes an essential aspect of the poem.

Free verse poetry that isn't dictated by an established form or meter, often influenced by the rhythms of speech.

Free verse describes poetry that does not follow a set metrical system or rhyme scheme. A rhythmic pattern of sound emerges in free-verse lines, yet there is no metrical plan in the composition used by the poet. Enjambment is often used in free-verse poetry, which frequently reflects the natural rhythms of speech. Poets from Walt Whitman to William Carlos Williams popularized the style in contemporary poetry. The opposite of free verse is formal verse, which adheres to a strict metric and rhyme system. Blank verse is poetry with a strict meter, but with no rhyme scheme.

See also form and meter.

Haiku a poem traditionally composed of three lines with 17 syllables, written in a 5/7/5 syllable count in English, and often focused on images from nature.

Haiku began in 13th-century Japan as the opening phrase of renga, an oral poem that was generally a hundred stanzas long and composed syllabically. The much shorter haiku broke away from renga in the 16th century and was mastered a century later by the poet Matsuo Basho. As the form evolved, many of its traditional traits—including its famous syllabic pattern—have been routinely broken. However, many elements of haiku have been preserved: the focus on a brief moment in time, the use of provocative and colorful images, the ability to be read in one breath, and the sense of sudden enlightenment.

Idiom a short expression peculiar to a language, people, or place that conveys a figurative meaning without a literal interpretation of the words used in the phrase.

From the late Latin *idioma*, which means "a peculiarity in language," idioms have been used for centuries. In French, *idiome* means a "form of speech peculiar to a people or place," and by the 1620s idiom also meant a "phrase or expression peculiar to a language." Idioms are set phrases and they only make sense if they are used exactly. Examples of idioms include a dime a dozen and piece of cake. Writers will use idioms to intensify an image, express an idea, or approximate everyday speech. William Shakespeare used idioms as a literary device in multiple works, including in Othello where jealousy is personified as the green-eyed monster.

Imagery language in a poem that represents a sensory experience.

Imagery uses vivid and figurative language to engage the senses and depict an object, person, scene, or feeling. The five types of imagery—visual, auditory, olfactory, tactile, and gustatory—relate to the five senses. Writers use imagery to build a specific sensory experience for readers to imagine and relate to. Literary devices such as simile and metaphor can be used to create imagery.

Line a fundamental unit in verse that carries meaning horizontally across the page and vertically from one line to the next.

A line in poetry is a group of words, most commonly arranged horizontally, that can vary in length and can adhere to a strict meter, or not. Lines determine a poem's syntax, tone, and rhythm. Understanding a line is a major element of understanding poetry, because a line's length and position relative to other lines help carry the meaning and music of a poem. A line that has strict meter is called a verse, or a metrical line of poetic composition.

See also meter.

List poem a deliberately organized poem containing a list of images or adjectives that build up to describe the poem's subject matter through an inventory of things.

List poetry, also known as catalog verse, is a poetic form and literary device that highlights an intentional catalog of people, places, things, and ideas in relation to each other, evoking an emotion or story. Its roots date back to roughly 100 AD when parts of the *Bible* were written. Verses of lists are also found in Homer's *Iliad*, which dates back to the early 8th or late 7th century BC. A list poem has no specific rhyme scheme or meter, and often features repetition, in particular anaphora. Famous examples include Walt Whitman's "I Hear America Singing" and "Song of Myself."

Lyric poetry non-narrative poetry that expresses the speaker's emotions and feelings, often with songlike qualities.

Lyric poetry began as a fixture of ancient Greece and was a popular form of poetry during the Greco-Roman era, as were dramas (written in verse) and epic poems. The lyric was far shorter, distinguished also by its focus on the poet's state of mind and personal themes rather than a clear narrative arc. Designed to be sung, lyric poems were typically accompanied by the lyre, a harp-like instrument from which lyric poetry derives its name. Today, lyric poetry encompasses a variety of forms in non-narrative poetry, including the sonnet, elegy, and ode.

See also ode and sonnet.

Metaphor a comparison between essentially unlike things or the application of a name or description to something to which it is not literally applicable.

Metaphor comes from the Greek word *metaphora* meaning "a transfer," in the sense of carrying over, altering, or changing the essence of one word to a different word. Metaphor is distinct from simile, another element of figurative language that compares two unlike things, in that metaphor does not use the words like or as in its comparison. Metaphor uses imagery to create a vivid picture by comparing two seemingly different things to each other, thus establishing a connection between the two.

Meter the measured pattern of rhythmic accents in a line of verse.

Meter, also known as metre, means the arrangement of language in measured rhythmic movements. The word comes from the Greek word *metron*, which means "measure." Meter is composed of a particular number of syllables found in a single line of poetry, and can be grouped into sets of two or three beats, also known as feet. Feet are units of stressed, also known as accented, syllables and unstressed or unaccented syllables.

Types of Feet in Poetry

Two-Syllables

Iamb: a metrical foot containing two syllables, the first of which is unstressed and the second of which is stressed (e.g., today).

Trochee: a metrical foot containing two syllables, the first of which is stressed and the second of which is unstressed (e.g., matter).

Spondee: a less common metrical foot in which two consecutive syllables are stressed (e.g., A.I.).

Three-Syllables

Anapest: a metrical foot containing three syllables, in which the first two are unstressed and the last is stressed (e.g., unaware).

Dactyl: a metrical foot containing three syllables, in which the first is stressed and the following two are unstressed (e.g., Waverly).

Each line of poetry has a number of feet, and meter refers to the number of feet used in a poetic line. Meter can vary or be consistent throughout a poem. Rising meter contains metrical feet that move from unstressed to stressed syllables, whereas falling meter contains metrical feet that move from stressed to unstressed syllables.

Types of Meter in Poetry

The length of poetic meter is described using Greek prefixes and suffixes:

Monometer – one foot, one beat per line

Dimeter – two feet, two beats per line

Trimeter – three feet, three beats per line

Tetrameter – four feet, four beats per line

Pentameter – five feet, five beats per line

Hexameter – six feet, six beats per line

Heptameter – seven feet, seven beats per line

Octameter – eight feet, eight beats per line

Nature poetry poetry that engages with, describes, or considers the natural world.

Nature poetry is a poetic genre popularized by the Romantic poets, including William Blake, John Keats, and William Wordsworth. Nature poetry expresses ideas, emotions, and situations that have to do with the natural world. There can also be a spiritual quality to nature poetry, as seen in the work of transcendentalist writers Ralph Waldo Emerson and Henry David Thoreau. Nature poems can be written in free verse or they can contain a specific meter and rhyme scheme. Environmental poetry is a modern extension of nature poetry, where contemporary poets writing about nature focus on environmental issues that address the adverse effects human actions have on the natural environment.

Nocturne a poem set at night.

Nocturne is from the French *nocturne*, meaning "composition appropriate to the evening or night." Similar to the musical composition, the nocturne is a poetic form that evokes feelings common to the night such as melancholy, reverie, prayer, sleeplessness, and solitude. Nocturnes are distinct from aubades, which are early morning songs that traditionally describe the parting of lovers. Nocturnes originated in the 17th century and continue to be used by contemporary poets to write about the night.

Ode a lyric address to an event, a person, or a thing not present.

Ode comes from the Greek *aeidein*, meaning to sing or chant, and belongs to the long and varied tradition of lyric poetry. Traditionally, odes were accompanied by music and dance; later odes became a favored poetic form of Romantic poets such as John Keats and William Wordsworth. There are three general types of odes: the Pindaric, Horatian, and Irregular. The Pindaric ode is named for the ancient Greek poet Pindar and contains a strict metrical structure throughout its three sections. The Horatian ode, named for the Roman poet Horace, also has a set metrical structure but tends to have a more intimate tone than a Pindaric ode. The Irregular ode follows no set metrical or rhyme system.

Pastoral a creative tradition, as well as individual work idealizing rural life and landscapes.

Viewed alternately as a genre, mode, or convention in literature, art, and music, the pastoral tradition can be traced to Hesiod, a Greek oral poet active between 750 and 650 BC, roughly the same time as Homer. The first written examples of pastoral literature are commonly attributed to the Greek poet Theocritus, who in the 3rd century BC wrote idylls, or short poems describing bucolic life. The conventions of the pastoral genre have evolved from idealized imagery about rural life to imagery that functions as a critique of industrialization and city life.

Persona poem a poem in which the poet assumes the voice of another person, fictional character, or identity.

Also known as a dramatic monologue, this form shares many characteristics of a theatrical monologue: an audience is implied; there is no dialogue; and the poet takes on the voice of a character, fictional identity, or persona. Because a dramatic monologue is by definition one person's speech, it is offered without overt analysis or commentary, placing emphasis on subjective qualities and leaving the reader to understand the speaker as they reveal their character and behavior throughout the poem. The dramatic monologue achieved its first era of distinction with the work of Victorian poet Robert Browning, whose deft mastery of the form remains unparalleled.

Personification the attribution of human qualities to animals, inanimate objects, or abstract ideas.

Personification has been used in poetry since ancient times, and Homer's *Iliad* and *Odyssey* include particularly fine early examples. Personification is often used in symbolic poetry or allegory, where animals or inanimate objects are endowed with human characteristics and tell a story, teach a lesson, or represent a different or deeper meaning. Personification was frequently used in the morality plays popular in the 15th and 16th centuries.

Poetic diction the language, including word choice and syntax, that sets poetry apart from other forms of writing.

Poetic diction describes the dialectic and linguistic styles used to write poetry. In some languages, poetic diction pertains more to the dialectal use and selection of words for poetic composition. Traditionally, in English poetry poetic diction mirrored elements of classical poetry, including the use of metaphors and the floral language that often accompanied descriptive imagery. According to Romantic poet William Wordsworth, poetic diction is the common language of the people in that it must be instinctive and spontaneous. Although Wordsworth strove to redefine poetic diction, modernist poets like Ezra Pound rejected poetic diction and renounced the use of superfluous language such as adjectives to ensure that a poem remained syntactically concise.

Praise poem a poem of tribute or gratitude.

Praise poetry is part of the literary tradition of many African and European cultures. For example, praise poems in Yorùbá are called *oriki*, in Zulu *isibongo*, and in Tswana *maboko*. In African literary tradition, a praise poem also refers to a series of laudatory epithets applied to gods, people, animals, places, etc., that captures the essence of being praised. These poems are an important part of an oral tradition, and professional bards—who may be both praise singers to a chief and court historians of their tribe—chant the poems. These poems offer imagery and storytelling related to a person or subject, and were also popular in medieval and Renaissance literature where praise poems expressed worship of or admiration for heroes, kings, or deities.

Quatrain a four-line stanza, or unit of four lines of verse, rhymed or unrhymed.

Quatrain is the diminutive of *quatre*, the French word for four. A quatrain, or four-line stanza, is commonly used in poetry, particularly in sonnets. Quatrains can be unrhymed or appear in rhyme schemes such as ABAB, where the first and third lines and the second and fourth lines rhyme. Other rhyme schemes for quatrains include AABA, AABB, ABBA, ABAC, and ABCB.

Four Examples of Quatrains in Poetry

Ballad – ABAB, written in iambic pentameter

Double Couplet – AABB

Envelope – ABBA

Heroic, also known as Elegiac – ABAB, written in iambic pentameter

See also line, meter, and stanza.

Repetition the poetic technique of repeating the same word or phrase multiple times within a poem.

Repetition is a literary device that predates writings from the 10th century BC. The recurrence of words or phrases throughout a poem influences the poem's tone, mood, rhythm, syntax, and structure. Repetition is found in free verse, but certain poetic forms such as the sestina or villanelle require the fundamental literary device.

Seven Examples of Repetition in Poetry

Anadiplosis – When a word or phrase is used at the end of one line or clause, and begins the next line or clause.

Anaphora – When a word or phrase is repeated at the beginning of each line or clause.

Antistrophe – When a word or phrase is repeated at the end of each line or clause.

Chiasmus – When a word or phrase is repeated in reverse order within a line or clause.

Epimone – When a word or phrase is repeated for the purpose of dwelling on an emotion; this device is usually used in dialogue.

Epizeuxis, also known as diacope – When words or phrases are repeated next to each other or in quick succession within a line or clause.

Symploce – When anaphora and antistrophe are used simultaneously, so a word or phrase is repeated at the beginning of each line or clause and that word or phrase is also repeated at the end of each line or clause.

Rhyme the correspondence of sounds in words or lines of verse.

Rhyme is often considered a defining feature of poetry, but it is a relatively new technique. The earliest surviving evidence of rhyming dates back to China in the 10th century BC. Rhymes are characterized by the syllables of the words and the placement of the words in a line or stanza. Perfect rhyme occurs if the words' final stressed vowel and all following sounds are identical. For example, bright and flight are perfect rhymes. Poetry usually uses end rhyme, the rhyming of the final syllables of a pair or group of lines. When two words in the same line rhyme, it's called internal rhyme. Poets might also use slant rhyme, which describes words that sound similar but don't exactly rhyme, such as young and long.

Sonnet a 14-line poem, traditionally written in iambic pentameter, that employs one of several rhyme schemes and adheres to a tightly structured thematic organization.

The sonnet is a popular classical form taken from the Italian *sonetto*, which means "a little sound or song." Two sonnet forms provide the model from which all other sonnets derive: the Petrarchan and the Shakespearean. The Petrarchan sonnet, named after the Italian poet Petrarch, is divided into two stanzas: an octave (the first eight lines) and an answering sestet (the final six lines). The rhyme scheme of the octave is typically ABBAABBA, while the sestet's rhyme scheme is typically CDECDE or CDCDCD, although other sestet variations exist. The Shakespearean sonnet, or English sonnet, consists of three quatrains and a couplet with the rhyme scheme ABAB, CDCD, EFEF, GG. Within the sonnet form, the volta plays a pivotal role, providing the turn and transition of the poem's tone and central themes.

Speaker the voice of a poem, similar to a narrator in fiction.

The speaker can be considered the storyteller or narrator of a poem. The narrative, emotions, and images in a poem are conveyed through the speaker. The poet might not necessarily be the speaker of the poem. Sometimes the poet will write from a different perspective or use the voice of a specific person, as in a persona poem. The term speaker clarifies the distinction between the poet's perspective and the perspective used in the poem. In some poems, the distinction between poet and speaker may not be obvious if there are no specific context clues to indicate that the voice narrating the poem has different characteristics from the person writing the poem.

Stanza a group of lines that form the basic unit of a poem.

In Italian, the word *stanza* means "room" or "standing, stopping place." Each stanza in a poem is a distinct unit like a room in a house. The number of lines in a stanza can vary, and each stanza within a poem typically has a specific tone and features. In free verse and contemporary poetry, a stanza resembles a prose paragraph in that it can also be used to mark a shift in mood, thought, and place. Stanzas are written according to Latin numerical values.

Types of Stanzas in Poetry

Monostich: One-line stanza

Couplet: Two-line stanza

Tercet: Three-line stanza

Quatrain: Four-line stanza

Quintet (also known as a quintain): Five-line stanza

Sestet: Six-line stanza

Septet: Seven-line stanza

Octave (also known as an octet): Eight-line stanza

Syllabic verse a poetic form that has a fixed or constrained number of syllables per line as well as per stanza.

The meter of syllabic verse poetry is determined by the number of syllables per line, rather than the number of stresses. Syllabic verse disregards the foot–meter system and is found in common poetic forms such as the haiku and tanka. Traditionally, syllabic verse was used in syllable-timed languages, such as French, Japanese, and Spanish, but not in stress-timed languages such as English and German. In the 20th century, British poets Robert Bridges, Elizabeth Daryush, and Dylan Thomas—among others—pioneered this poetic form. American poets who adopted syllabic verse as their standard metric system include James Laughlin and Marianne Moore.

Tone a literary device that conveys the author's attitude toward the subject, speaker, or audience of a poem.

All forms of writing have a tone. Tone is sometimes referred to as the mood of a poem, and can be established through figurative language and imagery. Tone in poetry can range from formal to informal, aggressive to defensive, sentimental to critical, and more. Tone allows the reader to better understand, and even relate to, the speaker's attitude toward the subject of a poem.

Translation the art of transferring meaning from one language to another.

Translation comes from the Latin *translatio*, which means "a transferring" or "a carrying over." Translation converts the meaning found in one language (the source language) to another language (the target language), paying close attention to the grammatical rules, vocabulary, and sentence structures of the text. Translation is a communication technology that can be a literal translation, or a freer one that brings the original text to life in the target language without losing any of the meaning and message found in the source language.

Volta a rhetorical shift that marks the change of a thought or argument in a poem.

Other common names for volta include turn, fulcrum, or hinge. The volta marks a shift from the main narrative or idea of the poem and awakens readers to a different meaning or to a reveal in the conclusion of the poem. Voltas are part of the sonnet form. In the Petrarchan sonnet, the volta occurs between the eighth and ninth lines. In the Shakespearean sonnet, the volta occurs before the final couplet. Voltas are also characteristics of other poetic forms, and can even occur in free verse poems.

4 Teaching with Primary Sources

Through Teach This Poem, the Academy of American Poets provides teachers with poems, primary sources, and classroom activities to help them engage their students with poetry in thought-provoking and innovative ways. The Library of Congress defines primary sources as "the raw materials of history—original documents and objects which were created at the time under study. They are different from secondary sources, accounts that retell, analyze, or interpret events, usually at a distance of time or place." In this workshop, participants will learn how to find original material to use alongside poems. These primary sources will help students to engage with the text and ask questions, all while honing their ability to observe and analyze both primary sources and poems.

Preparation

This workshop is best suited to a group, but it can also be completed individually. All participants will need access to a computer or tablet during the workshop for online searches. Facilitators should be prepared to display items on a screen or projector or provide hard copies of the material.

Time Required

Three hour-long sessions.

Featured Poem

The following poem can be used for the workshop exercises.

"Ozymandias"
by Percy Bysshe Shelley

I met a traveller from an antique land
Who said: "Two vast and trunkless legs of stone
Stand in the desert ... Near them, on the sand,
Half sunk, a shattered visage lies, whose frown,
And wrinkled lip, and sneer of cold command,
Tell that its sculptor well those passions read
Which yet survive, stamped on these lifeless things,
The hand that mocked them, and the heart that fed:
And on the pedestal these words appear:
'My name is Ozymandias, king of kings:
Look on my works, ye Mighty, and despair!'
Nothing beside remains. Round the decay
Of that colossal wreck, boundless and bare
The lone and level sands stretch far away."

Featured Primary Sources

The following c can be used as primary sources if participants use "Ozymandias" for the workshop exercises.

- *Entrance to the remains of the Temple of Aménophis flanked by headless statues of Ramses in Thebes*
- *Wady Saboua*
- *Monument*
- *Mount Rushmore, South Dakota, where living rock eternalizes the nation's progress*
- *Aerial view of Mount Rushmore, South Dakota*
- *Workmen on the face of Geo. Washington, Mt. Rushmore*

Participants are also encouraged to search for their own primary sources. In addition, participants should review the Library of Congress's "Teacher's Guide: Analyzing Primary Sources."

Part 1: Finding a Resource

The following exercises can be conducted individually or in pairs.

1. Pick a poem and circle the words in the poem that jump out at you. Is there a specific image that stands out? What primary emotion does the poem leave you with, and what in the poem makes you feel this way?
2. Make a two-column chart. On the left side, list the main words, images, and emotions that stood out to you in the poem. On the right side, list any search terms or resources that come to mind when thinking about the items in the left column. These could be songs, images, moments in history, aspects of everyday life, etc. How might these search terms relate to the poem?
3. Using the right side of your two-column chart, determine the keywords you will begin with as you conduct a search for potential resources to teach alongside the poem.
4. To search for resources, start by visiting the Library of Congress Teacher's Guide. Here are some examples of the many different ways to search the Library of Congress. Make sure to try several of them.

   - Search using the main search bar and try narrowing down your parameters by original format, date, location, and/or subject. If you also use the "available online" filter, you can guarantee that anything you find will be accessible.
   - Search for relevant topics by using Primary Source Sets on the Library of Congress's Classroom Materials page.
   - Search lesson plans by theme for relevant topics.

   - Run a site-specific search for Library of Congress content through Google and Google Images by typing "site: loc.gov [keyword]" into the Google search bar.
5. Collect four or five resources that you think would be interesting to teach alongside the poem you've chosen.

Part 2: Engaging Through Inquiry

You can complete the following exercises using the resources you've found yourself or the featured primary sources if using "Ozymandias."

1. Select one of the resources you found and analyze it alongside the Library of Congress's "Teacher's Guide: Analyzing Primary Sources." Make a note of any elements that prompt especially fruitful observations, conversations, or questions. What do you notice in the resource? What emotions or questions does it leave you with?
2. Read the poem again, keeping the resource you chose in mind. What did you notice in the poem that you didn't notice before? Does your analysis of the resource allow you to make any new observations or draw any comparisons to history, current events, or your own experiences? Which elements in the resource allowed you to make these leaps when reading the poem?
3. Develop a series of five questions to ask about the resource based on the "Teacher's Guide: Analyzing Primary Sources" and your own experience re-reading the poem. What questions might help students to observe, reflect on, and analyze the resource in ways that will best prepare them to encounter the poem?
4. Develop a series of questions to ask students about the poem. How might you help students shift their focus to the poem and encourage them to deploy the observation and analysis skills they used while engaging with the primary resource? How can you open up a discussion in innovative and interesting ways? Can any of the questions you asked about the resource be applied here as well?
5. If you're working individually, repeat this activity with each of the resources you identified in Part 1.

Part 3: Choosing the Best Resource

You can complete the following exercises using the resources you've found yourself or the featured primary sources provided for "Ozymandias."

1. If you're working in a group, take turns showing a resource to the other participants and asking the questions you have developed. If you're working alone, consider each resource and the developed questions in turn.
2. Think about how each resource generated unique conversations or individual thinking in relation to the poem.
   - How might the different resources encourage the participants to engage with the text?
   - Which resources could provide both an emotional and intellectual entry point to the poem?
   - Would any of the resources allow participants to make connections between the poem and their own lives or historical or current events?
   - Conversely, might any of the resources limit the discussion rather than open it up?
   - Could any resource move the discussion away from the poem entirely?
3. Discuss or think about which resource might work best to help students engage with the poem in a classroom setting and why. Are there any resources that would work particularly well if taught in tandem?

Incorporating primary sources into a lesson plan can equip students with accurate and personal insight into subjects both of the past and present. Providing opportunities for inference, evaluation, and critical thinking, these sources can enliven your experience teaching and bringing poetry into your classroom.

5 Adapting Teach This Poem to an Online or Hybrid Classroom

Academy of American Poets

Although Teach This Poem was developed with an in-person environment in mind, you can easily adapt it to an online or hybrid learning model. Please see the suggestions below to help you adjust these lessons to your environment as you see fit. Where applicable, we've made a distinction between synchronous and asynchronous meetings.

- Activities that require a white board: If you are meeting synchronously, you may wish to have participants type their answers into the chat section of a video meeting platform. For asynchronous meetings, you could send participants a poll or survey in advance and then share their answers in a word cloud.
- Activities that require participants to share images or items: For synchronous learning, you may want to ask participants to share their images via a video meeting platform at the same time. If you are meeting asynchronously, you could ask participants to post an image to your online platform.
- Activities that require partner work or small-group discussion: You can assign breakout groups using video meeting platforms in synchronous learning. If you are teaching asynchronously, we recommend that participants capture their thoughts in writing and share them with family members or friends when possible.
- Activities that require whole group discussion: For synchronous learning, participants can share their thoughts in a chat section or raise their hand. For asynchronous learning, consider dividing the lesson into several sessions. Participants can share their responses to the poem on a common platform such as a shared document or a group forum. You might also ask them to reply to at least one group member's response.

- Reading the poem: If you are meeting synchronously, we suggest sharing a video screen that allows participants to annotate together. If you are meeting asynchronously, we suggest asking participants to post their annotations on your online platform.
- Listening to the poem: For synchronous learning, look for audio of the poem to the right of its title on the poem's page on Poets.org. If no audio is available, you can ask two participants to read the poem. For asynchronous meetings, participants can look for the audio on Poets.org, read the poem aloud twice, or alternate reading with someone in their household.
- Activities that ask participants to write a poem or response: For synchronous and asynchronous meetings, you can create space on an online platform for participants to share their writing and respond to each other's work.
- Encourage your participants to create anthologies on Poets.org.

Poet and Translator Biographies

Sheila Black (1961–), born in Minneapolis, Minnesota, is the author of several poetry collections, including *Radium Dream* (Salmon Poetry, 2022) and *Iron, Ardent* (Educe Press, 2017). In 2000, she was the co-winner of the Frost-Pellicer Frontera Prize. Black is a cofounder of Zoeglossia, a nonprofit organization that promotes the work of poets with disabilities, and the director of development at the Association of Writers and Writing Programs (AWP). She lives in Texas.

Richard Blanco (1968–), born on February 15, 1968 in Madrid, is a poet, memoirist, and the Education Ambassador of the Academy of American Poets. He is the author of *Homeland of My Body: New and Selected Poems* (Beacon Press, 2023), among other works. Blanco has taught at various universities and is the distinguished visiting professor at Florida International University. In 2013, Blanco was selected to read at Barack Obama's second presidential inauguration. He was appointed Poet Laureate of Miami-Dade County in 2022 and was honored with the 2021 National Humanities Medal in 2023. He lives in Bethel, Maine.

Kai Carlson-Wee (1982–) is the author of *Rail* (BOA Editions, 2018). His work has appeared in *Best New Poets*, *New England Review*, *Gulf Coast*, and *The Missouri Review*, which awarded him the 2013 Editor's Prize. Carlson-Wee's photography has been featured in *Narrative Magazine*, and his poetry film *Riding the Highline* received a Jury Award at the 2015 Napa Valley Film Festival. A former Wallace Stegner Fellow, he lives in San Francisco and teaches at Stanford University.

Lucille Clifton (1936–2010), born on June 27, 1936 in Depew, New York, was a writer and author of several collections of poetry, including *Blessing the Boats: New and Selected Poems 1988–2000* (BOA Editions, 2000), which won the National Book Award, and *Good Woman: Poems and a Memoir 1969–1980* (BOA Editions, 1987), which was nominated for the Pulitzer Prize for Poetry. Her honors include a Lannan Literary Award, two fellowships from the National Endowment for the Arts, and the 2007 Ruth Lilly Prize. Clifton served as the poet laureate of Maryland from 1979 to 1985, and she was a Chancellor of the Academy of American Poets from 1999 to 2024. She died on February 13, 2010 at the age of 73.

E. E. Cummings (1894–1962) was born on October 14, 1894 in Cambridge, Massachusetts. His poetry collections include *Tulips and Chimneys* (1923), *is 5* (1926), and *95 poems* (1958). Cummings received two Guggenheim Fellowships, the 1958 Bollingen Prize for American Poetry, and a Ford Foundation grant. He served as the Charles Eliot Norton Professor at Harvard, At the time of his death on September 3, 1962, Cummings was the second most widely-read poet in the United States after Robert Frost.

Toi Derricotte (1941–) born on April 12, 1941 in Hamtramck, Michigan, is the author of eight books, including *I: New & Selected Poems* (University of Pittsburgh Press, 2019), winner of the 2020 Frost Award and finalist for the 2019 National Book Award in Poetry. Derricotte received the Distinguished Pioneering of the Arts Award from the Poetry Society of America and served as a Chancellor of the Academy of American Poets from 2011 to 2016. In 1996, Derricotte and poet Cornelius Eady co-founded the Cave Canem Foundation, a national poetry organization committed to nourishing the careers of African American poets. She is a professor emerita of English at the University of Pittsburgh.

Emily Dickinson (1830–1886), was born on December 10, 1830 in Amherst, Massachusetts. Although Dickinson was extremely prolific and regularly enclosed poems in letters to friends, she was not publicly recognized during her lifetime. She died in Amherst in 1886. Upon her death, Dickinson's family discovered 40 handbound volumes, or fascicles, that included almost 1,800 poems. The first volume of her work was published posthumously in 1890, and the original order of poems was not restored until 1981 with the work of Ralph W. Franklin.

Camille T. Dungy (1972–), born in 1972 in Denver, received an MFA from the University of North Carolina, Greensboro. She is a poet, an editor, and the author of various works including *Smith Blue* (Southern Illinois University Press, 2011), winner of the 2010 Crab Orchard Open Book Prize, and *Suck on the Marrow* (Red Hen Press, 2010), winner of an American Book Award, a California Book Award silver medal, and a Northern California Book Award. Dungy is a University Distinguished Professor at Colorado State University and lives in Fort Collins, Colorado.

Heid E. Erdrich (1963–), born in 1963 in Breckenridge, Minnesota, received a PhD from the Union Institute. She is the author of numerous collections, including *Little Big Bully* (Penguin Books, 2020), winner of the 2022 Rebekah Johnson Bobbitt National Prize for Poetry, and the editor of *New Poets of Native Nations* (Graywolf Press, 2018).

Erdrich directs Wiigwaas Press, an Ojibwe language publisher. She has received two Minnesota Book Awards, as well as honors from the National Poetry Series and the Native Arts and Cultures Foundation.

Ross Gay (1974–), born on August 1, 1974 in Youngstown, Ohio, received an MFA in poetry from Sarah Lawrence College and a PhD in English from Temple University. He is a poet and essayist, and the author of the poetry collection *Catalog of Unabashed Gratitude* (University of Pittsburgh Press, 2015), winner of the National Book Critics Circle Award and the Kingsley Tufts Poetry Award. Gay's honors include fellowships from Cave Canem and the Guggenheim Foundation. He teaches creative writing at Indiana University.

Reginald Gibbons (1947–), born in 1947 in Houston, earned his MA in English and creative writing and his PhD in comparative literature from Stanford University. He is the author of *Last Lake* (University of Chicago Press, 2016). His awards include the Folger Shakespeare Library's O.B. Hardison Jr. Poetry Prize, the John Masefield Award from the Poetry Society of America, and fellowships from the Guggenheim Foundation and the Fulbright Program. Gibbons has taught at Princeton University, Northwestern University, and Warren Wilson College.

Joy Harjo (1951–) is a member of the Mvskoke/Creek Nation and was born on May 9, 1951 in Tulsa, Oklahoma. She is a poet, musician, and playwright. In 1978, she received an MFA from the Iowa Writers Workshop. In 2019, Harjo became the first Native American to be appointed the United States poet laureate. She was elected Chancellor of the Academy of American Poets in 2019 and will serve through 2024. She is the author of numerous books of poetry, including *Weaving Sundown in a Scarlet Light: 50 Poems for 50 Years* (W. W. Norton, 2022). Harjo was awarded the 2023 Bollingen Prize for Poetry for *Weaving Sundown in a Scarlet Light* and in recognition of lifetime achievement in and contributions to American poetry. She lives in Tulsa, Oklahoma.

Linda Hogan (1947–), born in Denver, Colorado, in 1947, is the author of several works of prose and poetry, including *The Book of Medicines* (Coffee House Press, 1993), which received the Colorado Book Award and was a finalist for the National Book Critics Circle Award. Her first novel *Mean Spirit* (Atheneum, 1990) was a finalist for the 1991 Pulitzer Prize for Fiction. Her honors include a Lifetime Achievement Award from the Native Writers Circle of the Americas. Hogan lives in Colorado and is a professor emerita at the University of Colorado.

Gerard Manley Hopkins (1844–1889) was born on July 28, 1844 in Stratford, Essex, England. In 1867, he entered a Jesuit novitiate to become a priest, and burned the poetry he had written to date. Hopkins would not write poetry again until 1875 after the German ship *Deutschland* was wrecked at the mouth of the Thames River during a storm. In 1889, Hopkins died from typhoid fever and his poetry was published posthumously. Hopkins is widely considered to be one of the greatest Victorian poets, inspiring poets such as W. H. Auden, Dylan Thomas, and Charles Wright.

June Jordan (1936–2002) was born in New York City on July 9, 1936 and attended Barnard College. She was an activist, poet, writer, teacher, and prominent figure in the civil rights, feminist, antiwar, and LGBTQ movements of the 20th century. Jordan's numerous books of poetry include *Directed by Desire: The Collected Poems* (Copper Canyon Press, 2007). Jordan received a Rockefeller Foundation grant and taught at the University of California, Berkeley where she founded Poetry for the People. Jordan died on June 14, 2002 in Berkeley, California.

Galway Kinnell (1927–2014) was born in Providence, Rhode Island, on February 1, 1927. In 1948, Kinnell received a master's degree from the University of Rochester. Kinnell's volumes of poetry include *The Book of Nightmares* (Houghton Mifflin, 1971) and *A New Selected Poems* (Houghton Mifflin, 2000), a finalist for the National Book Award. Among other honors, he received a MacArthur Fellowship and the 2002 Frost Medal from the Poetry Society of America. Kinnel was a Chancellor of the Academy of American Poets from 2001 to 2006. He died in Sheffield, Vermont, on October 28, 2014.

Joseph O. Legaspi (1971–) was born in the Philippines, where he lived before immigrating to Los Angeles with his family at age 12. He received an MFA from New York University's Creative Writing Program. Legaspi is the author of *Imago* (CavanKerry Press, 2007), winner of a Global Filipino Literary Award. In 2004, he co-founded Kundiman, a national organization serving Asian American writers and readers. He works at Columbia University, and lives in Queens, New York.

Denise Levertov (1923–1997) was born in Ilford, Essex, England, on October 24, 1923 and became an important voice in the American avant-garde with the American publication of *Here and Now* (City Lights, 1956). She went on to publish more than 20 volumes of poetry, including *With Eyes at the Back of our Heads* (New Directions, 1959) and *The Freeing of the Dust* (New Directions, 1975), which won the Lenore Marshall Poetry Prize. Levertov died on December 20, 1997.

Ada Limón (1976–), born on March 28, 1976 in Sonoma, California, received an MFA in poetry from New York University. Limón's first collection of poetry, *Lucky Wreck* (Autumn House Press, 2006), was the winner of the 2005 Autumn House Poetry Prize and *Bright Dead Things* (Milkweed Editions, 2015) was a finalist for the National Book Award. A Guggenheim Fellow, Limón has also received a grant from the New York Foundation for the Arts. In 2022, she was appointed to serve as the United States poet laureate.

Poet and Translator Biographies

Layli Long Soldier (1972–) received a BFA from the Institute of American Indian Arts and an MFA from Bard College. She is the author of *WHEREAS* (Graywolf Press, 2017), which won the 2018 PEN/Jean Stein Book Award and was short-listed for the National Book Award. Long Soldier has received a Lannan Literary Fellowship, a National Artist Fellowship from the Native Arts and Cultures Foundation, and a Whiting Award.

Ricardo Alberto Maldonado (1981–) born and raised in Puerto Rico, is a graduate of Tufts and Columbia University's School of the Arts. He is a poet, translator, editor, and author of *The Life Assignment* (Four Way Books, 2020). Maldonado is the board chair of the Poetry Project, and serves on the board of directors of the New York Foundation for the Arts. He is the Academy of American Poets' President and Executive Director.

Campbell McGrath (1962–), born in Chicago in 1962, received his MFA in creative writing from Columbia University. He is the author of 11 collections of poetry, including *Nouns & Verbs: New and Selected Poems* (Ecco Press, 2019) and *Spring Comes to Chicago* (Ecco Press, 1996), which won the Kingsley Tufts Poetry Award. McGrath's honors include a MacArthur Foundation Fellowship, a Guggenheim Fellowship, and the Witter Bynner Fellowship from the Library of Congress.

Claude McKay (1889–1948) was born Festus Claudius McKay in Sunny Ville, Jamaica, on September 15, 1889. McKay is a prominent figure of the Harlem Renaissance movement, and the author of *Harlem Shadows* (1922), *Constab Ballads* (1912), and *Songs of Jamaica* (1912), among many other books of poetry and prose. During the 1920s, he aligned himself with the United Negro Improvement Association (UNIA). In 1934, McKay moved back to the United States and lived in Harlem, New York. McKay then left for Chicago in September 1946 and died on May 22, 1948.

Marianne Moore (1887–1972) was born near St. Louis, Missouri, on November 15, 1887, and in 1918 she and her mother moved to New York City. In 1921, Moore's first book *Poems* was published by The Egoist Press without her knowledge or consent. Moore served as an editor at *The Dial* from 1925 to 1929. Her many honors include the Bollingen Prize for American Poetry, the National Book Award for Poetry, and the Pulitzer Prize for Poetry. Moore died in New York City on February 5, 1972.

Margaret Noodin (1965–) is the author of *Gijigijigaaneshi Gikendaan* (Wayne State University Press, 2020) and *Weweni* (Wayne State University Press, 2015), both collections of bilingual poems in Anishinaabemowin and English, as well as *Bawaajimo: A Dialect of Dreams in Anishinaabe Language and Literature* (Michigan State University Press, 2014). Noodin is a professor of English and American Indian studies at the University of Wisconsin–Milwaukee.

Poet and Translator Biographies

Naomi Shihab Nye (1952–) was born on March 12, 1952 in St. Louis, Missouri. She is the author of numerous collections of poetry, including *You and Yours* (BOA Editions, 2005), which received the Isabella Gardner Poetry Award. She is also the author of several children's books, including *Habibi* (Simon Pulse, 1997), which won the Jane Addams Children's Book Award. Nye served as a Chancellor of the Academy of American Poets from 2009 to 2014 and she received the 2019 Ivan Sandrof Award for lifetime achievement. She currently lives in San Antonio, Texas.

Matthew Olzmann (1976–) was born in Detroit, Michigan. He received a BA from the University of Michigan–Dearborn and an MFA from Warren Wilson College. He is the author of *Constellation Route* (Alice James Books, 2022), *Contradictions in the Design* (Alice James Books, 2016), and *Mezzanines* (Alice James Books, 2013), winner of the 2011 Kundiman Poetry Prize. Olzmann has received fellowships from the Kresge Foundation and Kundiman. He teaches at Dartmouth College and lives in Vermont.

January Gill O'Neil (1969–), born in Norfolk, Virginia, received an MFA from New York University and is the author of *Rewilding* (CavanKerry Press, 2018) and *Misery Islands* (CavanKerry Press, 2014), winner of a 2015 Paterson Award for Literary Excellence. O'Neil is the recipient of a fellowship from Cave Canem and a grant from the Barbara Deming Memorial Fund. She is an associate professor of English at Salem State University and lives in Beverly, Massachusetts.

Alexander Posey (1873–1908), born August 3, 1873, was a Muskogee Creek poet, journalist, and humorist known for his poems and Fus Fixico letters, a series of satirical letters written from the perspective of his fictional persona Fus Fixico that commented on local and national politics of the time. He served as the editor for the *Eufaula Indian Journal* before passing away on May 27, 1908. *The Poems of Alexander Lawrence Posey* (Crane Printers), collected and arranged by Posey's wife, was published posthumously in 1910.

Lois Red Elk (1940–) is an enrolled member of the Fort Peck Sioux. She is the author of *Why I Return to Makoce* (Many Voices Press, 2015), *Dragonfly Weather* (Lost Horse Press, 2013), and *Our Blood Remembers* (Many Voices Press, 2011), which received the Best Nonfiction Award from the Wordcraft Circle of Native Writers and Storytellers. Red Elk has previously worked as an actor and technical advisor for numerous Hollywood film productions. She teaches cultural courses and traditional language classes at Fort Peck Community College in Montana.

Alberto Ríos (1952–), born on September 18, 1952 in Nogales, Arizona, is a poet, memoirist, and novelist. His poetry collections include *The Theater of Night* (Copper Canyon Press, 2005), winner of the 2007 PEN/Beyond Margins Award, and *The Smallest Muscle in the Human Body* (Copper Canyon Press, 2002), a finalist for the National Book

Award. Ríos was a Chancellor of the Academy of American Poets from 2013 to 2018. He is a Regents Professor at Arizona State University and serves as Arizona's inaugural poet laureate.

Arthur Sze (1950–) was born in New York City in 1950. He is a poet, translator, and editor and the author of 11 books of poetry, including *The Glass Constellation* (Copper Canyon Press, 2021). Sze was awarded the Poetry Foundation's Ruth Lilly Prize in 2022 and is the recipient of many other awards and honors. He served as a Chancellor of the Academy of American Poets from 2011 to 2016. Sze is a professor emeritus at the Institute of American Indian Arts and was the first poet laureate of Santa Fe, New Mexico, where he lives.

Miguel de Unamuno (1864–1936) was born on September 29, 1864 in the Basque city of Bilbao, Spain. He was a poet, novelist, and playwright. De Unamuno received a PhD from the University of Madrid in 1884 and did not begin to publish poetry until the age of 43. His poetry collections include *Poesías* (Poetry, 1907), *Rosario de sonetos lícos* (Rosary of Sonnets, 1911), and *El Cristo de Velasquez* (The Christ of Velasquez, 1920). De Unamuno died on New Year's Eve in 1936.

Afaa Michael Weaver (1951–), born Michael S. Weaver in Baltimore, Maryland, in 1951, is a poet, playwright, and fiction writer. Weaver took the name Afaa in 1997 after the death of his first child; the name, given to him by the Nigerian playwright Tess Onwueme, is an Ibo word meaning "oracle." He has published several collections of poetry, including *The Government of Nature* (University of Pittsburgh Press, 2013), which won the Kingsley Tufts Poetry Award. Weaver has received numerous fellowships and awards. He lives in Connecticut.

Walt Whitman (1819–1892) was born on May 31, 1819 in West Hills, New York, and attended Brooklyn public schools as a child. During his lifetime, Whitman refined his poetry collection *Leaves of Grass*, publishing several editions with additions and revisions. He spent his declining years preparing his final volume of poems and prose, *Good-Bye My Fancy* (David McKay, 1891). Whitman died on March 26, 1892.

William Carlos Williams (1883–1963) was born on September 17, 1883 in Rutherford, New Jersey. He received his MD from the University of Pennsylvania and sustained a medical practice throughout his life. He also had a prolific career as a poet, novelist, essayist, and playwright. His major works include *Imaginations* (New Directions, 1970) and *Pictures from Brueghel and Other Poems* (New Directions, 1962), which was awarded the Pulitzer Prize for Poetry. Williams died in New Jersey on March 4, 1963.

Bibliography

111th Congress. "111th Congress 1st Session: S. J. Res. 14," April 30, 2009. https://www.congress.gov/111/bills/sjres14/BILLS-111sjres14is.pdf

Academy of American Poets. "A Brief Guide to Imagism | Academy of American Poets." Poets.org. Academy of American Poets, September 5, 2017. https://poets.org/text/brief-guide-imagism

———. "A Brief Guide to Imagism | Academy of American Poets." Poets.org. Academy of American Poets,. "An Interview with Education Ambassador Richard Blanco." Poets.org. Academy of American Poets, April 12, 2023. https://poets.org/text/interview-education-ambassador-richard-blanco

———. "An Interview with Joy Harjo, U.S. Poet Laureate." Poets.org. Academy of American Poets, April 1, 2019. https://poets.org/text/interview-joy-harjo-us-poet-laureate

———. "Emily Dickinson Discussion Questions." Poets.org. Academy of American Poets. n.d.-a https://poets.org/text/emily-dickinson-discussion-questions

———. "From the Archive: June Jordan's 1978 Postcard." Poets.org. Academy of American Poets. n.d.-b https://poets.org/text/archive-june-jordans-1978-postcard

———. "November 2022 Poem-a-Day Guest Editor Jake Skeets." Poets.org. Academy of American Poets. n.d.-c https://poets.org/November-2022-poem-a-day-guest-editor-jake-skeets

———. "Poets Laureate Fellows Interviews: B. K. Fischer." Poets.org. Academy of American Poets, December 20, 2022. https://poets.org/text/poets-laureate-fellows-interviews-b-k-fischer

———. "Teach This Poem: Poetry to the Rescue!" Poets.org. Academy of American Poets. https://poets.org/teach-poem-poetry-rescue

Baker, Al, J. David Goodman, and Benjamin Mueller. "Beyond the Chokehold: The Path to Eric Garner's Death." *The New York Times*, June 13, 2015. https://www.nytimes.com/2015/06/14/nyregion/eric-garner-police-chokehold-staten-island.html

Bibliography

Beck, Julie. "The Psychology of Home: Why Where You Live Means so Much." *The Atlantic*, December 30, 2011. https://www.theatlantic.com/health/archive/2011/12/the-psychology-of-home-why-where-you-live-means-so-much/249800/

Bolle Kees, W., Jonathan Z. Smith, and Richard G. A. Buxton. "Myth." In *Encyclopædia Britannica*, September 5, 2023. https://www.britannica.com/topic/myth

Cass White, Heather. "The Marianne Moore of First Intentions." Poets.org. Academy of American Poets, June 18, 2018. https://poets.org/text/marianne-moore-first-intentions

Cleveland, Claire, and Andrea Dukakis. "Yes, It Really Is Quieter When It Snows. Here's the Science behind the Calm after the Storm." Colorado Public Radio, February 4, 2020. https://www.cpr.org/2020/02/04/yes-it-really-is-quieter-when-it-snows-heres-the-science-behind-the-calm-after-the-storm/#:~:text=One%20study%20found%20a%20couple

Curie, Irène, and Marie Curie. "Marie Curie and Irène Curie on Radium | Britannica." In *Encyclopædia Britannica*, n.d. https://www.britannica.com/topic/Marie-Curie-and-Irene-Curie-on-radium-1983710

Derricotte, Toi. "The Bond of Living Things: Poems of Ancestry." Poets.org. Academy of American Poets, May 12, 2005. https://poets.org/text/bond-living-things-poems-ancestry

Dewey, John. *Art as Experience*, 18th ed. New York City: Perigee Books, 1980.

Diaz, Natalie. "A Poetry Portfolio: Featuring Five of Our Country's Finest Native Poets." Poets.org. Academy of American Poets, November 10, 2015. https://poets.org/text/poetry-portfolio-featuring-five-our-countrys-finest-native-poets

Doty, Mark. "Tide of Voices: Why Poetry Matters Now." Poets.org. Academy of American Poets. August 9, 2010. https://poets.org/text/tide-voices-why-poetry-matters-now

Encyclopedia Britannica. "Personification." *Encyclopedia Britannica*, n.d. https://www.britannica.com/art/personification

Fox, M. W. "Empathy, Humaneness and Animal Welfare." Edited by M. W. Fox and L. D. Mickley. WellBeing International. The Humane Society of the United States, 1984. https://www.wellbeingintlstudiesrepository.org/cgi/viewcontent.cgi?article=1000&context=acwp_habr

Greene, Maxine. *Variations on a Blue Guitar: The Lincoln Center Institute Lectures on Aesthetic Education*. New York and London: Teachers College Press, 2018.

Harjo, Joy. "Ancestors: A Mapping of Indigenous Poetry and Poets." Poets.org. Academy of American Poets, November 24, 2015.

Harvey, Chelsea. "How Climate Change May Affect Winter 'Weather Whiplash.'" *Scientific American*. E&E News, February 11, 2019. https://www.scientificamerican.com/article/how-climate-change-may-affect-winter-weather-whiplash/

Hersher, Rebecca. "Mae Keane, One of the Last 'Radium Girls,' Dies at 107." NPR, December 28, 2014. https://www.npr.org/2014/12/28/373510029/saved-by-a-bad-taste-one-of-the-last-radium-girls-dies-at-107?mc_cid=37859fa1d8&mc_eid=UNIQID

Hirsch, Edward. "How to Read a Poem." Academy of American Poets and the Great Books Foundation. https://poets.org/text/how-read-poem-0

Hirshfield, Jane. *Ten Windows: How Great Poems Transform the World*. New York City: Alfred A. Knopf, Inc., 2015.

Hughes, Langston. "The Ceaseless Rings of Walt Whitman." Poets.org. Academy of American Poets, April 22, 2019. https://poets.org/text/ceaseless-rings-walt-whitman

Lanham, Joseph Drew. "Kinship of Clay." Poets.org. Academy of American Poets, June 16, 2023. https://poets.org/text/kinship-clay

Library of Congress. "Removing Native Americans from Their Land." Library of Congress, 2021. https://www.loc.gov/classroom-materials/immigration/native-american/removing-native-americans-from-their-land/

Limón, Ada. "Video: Ada Limón Reads 'Marketing Life for Those of Us Left'." Poets.org. Academy of American Poets, October 15, 2010. https://poets.org/text/video-ada-limon-reads-marketing-life-those-us-left

Lorde, Audre. *Conversations with Audre Lorde*. Edited by Joan Wylie Hall. The University Press of Mississippi, 2004.

Lycurgus, Cate. "Also a Kind of Love: An Interview with Camille Dungy." 32 Poems. https://32poems.com/prose/also-a-kind-of-love-an-interview-with-camille-dungy-by-cate-lycurgus/

Massachusetts Institute of Technology. "An Introduction to the Physics of Sailing." MIT Blossoms. Massachusetts Institute of Technology. https://blossoms.mit.edu/videos/lessons/introduction_physics_sailing

Oceana International. "Ocean Animal Encyclopedia." Oceana. Oceana International, n.d. https://oceana.org/marine-life/

Ojibwe People's Dictionary. "The Ojibwe People's Dictionary." Umn.edu, n.d. https://ojibwe.lib.umn.edu/

O'Neill, Natasha. "NASA's James Webb Telescope Shows Many Stars in Southern Ring Nebula." CTVNews, January 31, 2023. https://www.ctvnews.ca/sci-tech/nasa-s-james-webb-telescope-shows-many-stars-in-southern-ring-nebula-1.6253659

Ríos, Alberto. "Some Thoughts on the Integrity of the Single Line in Poetry." Poets.org. Academy of American Poets, February 20, 2011. https://poets.org/text/some-thoughts-integrity-single-line-poetry

The Library of Congress. "Getting Started with Primary Sources," n.d. https://www.loc.gov/programs/teachers/getting-started-with-primary-sources/

Shelley, Percy Bysshe. "Ozymandias." *From Rosalind and Helen, A Modern Eclogue; With Other Poems* (C. and J. Ollier, 1819) by Percy Bysshe Shelley, edited by H. Buxton Forman. This poem is in the public domain.

Shihab Nye, Naomi. "Video: Naomi Shihab Nye on Inspiration." Poets.org. Academy of American Poets, July 26, 2011. https://poets.org/text/video-naomi-shihab-nye-inspiration

U.S. Department of Agriculture, and U.S. Forest Service. "Anatomy of a Tree," n.d. https://www.fs.usda.gov/learn/trees/anatomy-of-tree

U.S. Department of the Interior. "10 Public Lands with Powerful Native American Connections, U.S. Department of the Interior." Web.archive.org, October 30, 2020. https://web.archive.org/web/20230207222645; https://www.doi.gov/blog/10-public-lands-powerful-native-american-connections

United States Environmental Protection Agency. "Learn about Environmental Justice." US EPA, November 7, 2018. https://www.epa.gov/environmentaljustice/learn-about-environmental-justice

Credits

Sheila Black, "Radium Dream," from *Radium Dream* (Salmon Poetry, 2022) by Sheila Black. Copyright © 2022 by Sheila Black. Used with the permission of Salmon Poetry.

Richard Blanco, "Complaint of El Río Grande," from *How to Love a Country: Poems* (Beacon Press, 2019) by Richard Blanco. Copyright © 2019 by Richard Blanco. Used with the permission of Beacon Press, Boston Massachusetts.

Kai Carlson-Wee, "Bracken." Copyright © 2018 Kai Carlson-Wee. This poem originally appeared in *Tin House*, Winter 2018. Used with the permission of the author.

Lucille Clifton, "blessing the boats," from *Blessing the Boats* (Penguin Classics, 2000) by Lucille Clifton. Copyright © 2000 by Lucille Clifton. Used with the permission of Penguin Books Limited.

E. E. Cummings, "maggie and milly and molly and may," from *The Complete Poems: 1904–1962* (Liveright, 2016) by E. E. Cummings, edited by George J. Firmage. Copyright © 1956, 1984, 1991, 2016 by the Trustees for the E. E. Cummings Trust. Used with the permission of Liveright Publishing Corporation.

Toi Derricotte, "Cherry Blossoms," from *The Undertaker's Daughter* (University of Pittsburgh Press, 2011) by Toi Derricotte. Copyright © 2011 by Toi Derricotte. Used with the permission of the University of Pittsburgh Press.

Emily Dickinson, "There is no frigate like a book (1263)," from Poems (Little Brown, and Co., 1911) by Emily Dickinson, edited by Mabel Loomis Todd. This poem is in the public domain.

Camille T. Dungy, "Characteristics of Life," from Trophic Cascade (Wesleyan University Press, 2017) by Camille Dungy. Copyright © 2017 by Camille Dungy. Used with the permission of Wesleyan University Press.

Heid E. Erdrich, "Peace Path." Copyright © 2016 by Heid E. Erdrich. Used with the permission of the author.

Ross Gay, "A Small Needful Fact," originally published through Split This Rock's The Quarry: A Social Justice Poetry Database. Copyright © 2015 by Ross Gay. Used with the permission of the author.

Reginald Gibbons, "In cold spring air," from Creatures of a Day (LSU Press, 2008) by Reginald Gibbons. Copyright © 2008 by Reginald Gibbons. Used with the permission of LSU Press.

Joy Harjo, "Remember," from She Had Some Horses (W. W. Norton & Company, Inc., 1983) by Joy Harjo. Copyright © 1983 by Joy Harjo. Used with the permission of W. W. Norton & Company, Inc.

Linda Hogan, "Map," from Dark. Sweet.: New & Selected Poems (Coffee House Press, 1993) by Linda Hogan. Copyright © 1993 by Linda Hogan. Used with the permission of The Permissions Company, LLC on behalf of Coffee House Press, coffeehousepress.org.

Gerard Manley Hopkins, "Binsey Poplars" from Poems of Gerard Manley Hopkins, First Edition (Humphrey Milford, 1918) by Gerard Manley Hopkins, edited by Robert Bridges. This poem is in the public domain.

June Jordan, "These Poems," from We're On: A June Jordan Reader (Alice James Books, 2017) by June Jordan. Copyright © 2017 by June Jordan. All rights reserved. Used with the permission of The Frances Goldin Literary Agency.

Galway Kinnell, "Saint Francis and the Sow," from A New Selected Poems by Galway Kinnell (Houghton Mifflin, 2000). Copyright © 2000 by Galway Kinnell. Used with the permission of HarperCollins Publishers.

Joseph O. Legaspi, "The Tree Sparrows," originally published in Orion Magazine. Copyright © 2016 by Joseph O. Legaspi. Used with the permission of the author.

Denise Levertov, "The Metier of Blossoming," from This Great Unknowing (New Directions, 1998) by Denise Levertov. Copyright © 1998 by The Denise Levertov Literary Trust, Paul A. Lacey and Valerie Trueblood Rapport, co-trustees. Used with the permission of New Directions Publishing Corp.

Ada Limón, "Dead Stars" and "Instructions on Not Giving Up," from The Carrying (Milkweed Editions, 2018) by Ada Limón. Copyright © 2018 by Ada Limón. Reprinted with the permission of The Permissions Company, LLC on behalf of Milkweed Editions, milkweed.org.

Layli Long Soldier, "from WHEREAS ["WHEREAS when offered…"], from Whereas (Graywolf Press, 2017). Copyright © 2017 by Layli Long Soldier. Used with the permission of The Permissions Company, LLC on behalf of Graywolf Press, Minneapolis, Minnesota, graywolfpress.org.

Credits

Campbell McGrath, "The Everglades." Copyright © 2016 by Campbell McGrath. Used with the permission of the author.

Claude McKay, "To Winter" from Spring in New Hampshire and Other Poems (Grant Richards LTD, 1920) by Claude McKay. This poem is in the public domain.

Marianne Moore, "Poetry," from Others for 1919: An Anthology of the New Verse (Nicholas L. Brown, 1920), edited by Alfred Kreymborg. This poem is in the public domain.

Margaret Noodin, "Nimbawaadaan Akiing / I Dream a World." Copyright © 2021 by Margaret Noodin. Used with the permission of the author.

Naomi Shihab Nye, "Valentine for Ernest Mann," from Red Suitcase (BOA Editions, Ltd., 1994) by Naomi Shihab Nye. Copyright © 1994 by Naomi Shihab Nye. Used with the permission of the author.

Matthew Olzmann, "Letter to Someone Living Fifty Years from Now," from Constellation Route (Alice James Books, 2022) by Matthew Olzmann. Copyright © 2022 by Matthew Olzmann. Reprinted with the permission of The Permissions Company, LLC on behalf of Alice James Books, alicejamesbooks.org.

January Gill O'Neil, "In Praise of Okra" from Underlife (CavanKerry Press, 2009) by January Gill O'Neil. Copyright © 2009 by January Gill O'Neil. Reprinted with the permission of The Permissions Company, LLC on behalf of CavanKerry Press, Ltd., www.cavankerry.org.

Alexander Posey, "Coyote," from The Poems of Alexander Lawrence Posey (Crane & Company, Printers, 1910) by Alexander Posey, edited by Mrs. Minnie H. Posey with a memoir by William Elsely Connelley. This poem is in the public domain.

Lois Red Elk, "She Was Fed Turtle Soup," from Why I Return to Makoce (Many Voices Press, 2015) by Lois Red Elk. Copyright © 2015 by Lois Red Elk. Used with the permission of the author.

Alberto Ríos, "On Gathering Artists" from A Small Story About the Sky (Copper Canyon Press, 2015). Copyright © 2015 by Alberto Ríos. Reprinted with the permission of The Permissions Company, LLC on behalf of Copper Canyon Press, coppercanyonpress.org.

Arthur Sze, "The Shapes of Leaves" from The Redshifting Web: Poems 1970–1998 (Copper Canyon Press, 1972). Copyright © 1972 by Arthur Sze. Reprinted with the permission of The Permissions Company, LLC on behalf of Copper Canyon Press, coppercanyonpress.org.

Miguel de Unamuno, "La nevada es silenciosa / The Snowfall Is So Silent," from Rimas de dentro (Talleres Tipográficos Cuesta, 1923) by Miguel de Unamuno. Translated from the Spanish by Ricardo Alberto Maldonado. The untranslated poem is in the public domain.

Afaa Michael Weaver, "The Silver Thread." Copyright © 2017 by Afaa Michael Weaver. Used with the permission of the author.

Walt Whitman, "The Indications [excerpt]," from Leaves of Grass (David McKay, 1900) by Walt Whitman. This poem is in the public domain.

William Carlos Williams, "Willow Poem," from Sour Grapes (The Four Seas Company, 1921) by William Carlos Williams. This poem is in the public domain.

Acknowledgments

Teach This Poem would not have existed without the Academy of American Poets, including the Board of Directors, Chancellors, Education Advisory Council, and Academy staff past and present, and their dedication and work to fund, support, and produce this important resource year in and out.

The series owes a great deal of gratitude to Jen Benka, former Executive Director and President of the Academy, whose leadership inspired and encouraged me. Mary Gannon, the former Associate Director/Director of Content, made the early concept of Teach This Poem possible, and, with Jen, recognized the importance of a print collection of this work. Ansley Moon most ably took over the creation of online lessons in 2019.

Teach This Poem could not have begun without the dedication and feedback from a group of New York City third and fourth grade school teachers, as well as teachers from high schools connected with New Visions for Public Schools. They grounded our ideas and inspired us with their commitment to teach poetry to their students.

Present Academy Staff Members Kat Rejsek, Thea Matthews, and Jeffery Gleaves, as well as Academy Board Member Alexandra Jackson and former Staff Member Emma Hine, lent their talents and diligence to the book's production. Ricardo Alberto Maldonado, the Academy's current Executive Director and President, provided support and encouragement.

And Richard Blanco, the Education Ambassador for the Academy, was, and continues to be, an invaluable and supportive colleague.

My greatest thanks to you all.

Author Biography

Madeleine Fuchs Holzer was the inaugural Educator in Residence at the Academy of American Poets from 2014 to 2023. She previously served as Educational Development Director and Program Development Director at Lincoln Center Institute for the Arts in Education, where she wrote the Institute's Capacities for Imaginative Learning and other conceptual documents. Prior to that, Holzer was the Director of Arts in Education at the New York State Council on the Arts. Her poetry and essays have been published in *Education Week*, *Black Fly Review, Footwork: Paterson Literary Review*, and *Pearl*, among others. Holzer has taught at Cornell and New York Universities, and at Fox Lane High School in Bedford, New York. In addition, she taught poetry at East Side Community High School in New York City. She was Senior Editor for English/Language Arts at Sunburst Communications, where she developed the award-winning CD-ROMs *Romeo and Juliet: Center Stage* and *In My Own Voice: Multicultural Poets on Identity*. Holzer holds an EdD from Teachers College, Columbia University, and an MA in English with a concentration in creative writing from New York University. She was a Resident at MacDowell.

For Product Safety Concerns and Information please contact our EU
representative GPSR@taylorandfrancis.com
Taylor & Francis Verlag GmbH, Kaufingerstraße 24, 80331 München, Germany

www.ingramcontent.com/pod-product-compliance
Lightning Source LLC
Chambersburg PA
CBHW080520300426
44112CB00018B/2800